Social Research Perspectives

Occasional Reports on Current Topics

12

Risk Management
and Political Culture

A Comparative Study of Science
in the Policy Context

by Sheila Jasanoff

RUSSELL SAGE FOUNDATION   NEW YORK

The Russell Sage Foundation

The Russell Sage Foundation, one of the oldest of America's general purpose foundations, was established in 1907 by Mrs. Margaret Olivia Sage for "the improvement of social and living conditions in the United States." The Foundation seeks to fulfill this mandate by fostering the development and dissemination of knowledge about the political, social, and economic problems of America. It conducts research in the social sciences and public policy, and publishes books and pamphlets that derive from this research.

The Board of Trustees is responsible for oversight and the general policies of the Foundation, while administrative direction of the program and staff is vested in the President, assisted by the officers and staff. The President bears final responsibility for the decision to publish a manuscript as a Russell Sage Foundation book. In reaching a judgment on the competence, accuracy, and objectivity of each study, the President is advised by the staff and selected expert readers. The conclusions and interpretations in Russell Sage Foundation publications are those of the authors and not of the Foundation, its Trustees, or its staff. Publication by the Foundation, therefore, does not imply endorsement of the contents of the study.

Library of Congress Cataloging-in-Publication Data

Jasanoff, Sheila,
   Risk management and political culture.

   (Social research perspectives: occasional reports
on current topics; 12)
   1. Health risk assessment—Government policy.
2. Risk management—Government policy.   3. Carcinogens.
I. Title.   II. Series: Social research perspectives; 12.
RA566.27.J37   1986   363.1   86-6443
ISBN 0-87154-408-3

NOTICE of series title change: *Social Research Perspectives* is a new title for the *Social Science Frontiers* series (volumes 1–9 published 1969–1977). The numbering of *Perspectives* volumes is a continuation of the *Frontiers* numbering.

10 9 8 7 6 5 4 3 2 1

Social Research Perspectives

Occasional Reports on Current Topics from the Russell Sage Foundation

The *Social Research Perspectives* series revives a special format used by the Russell Sage Foundation for nine volumes published from 1969 to 1977 under the series title, *Social Science Frontiers*. The *Frontiers* series established itself as a valuable source of information about significant developments in the social sciences.

With the re-named *Perspectives* series, we again provide a timely, flexible, and accessible outlet for the products of ongoing social research—from literature reviews to explorations of emerging issues and new methodologies; from summaries of current policy to agendas for future study and action.

The following *Frontiers* titles are still available:

Now available in the *Perspectives* series:

Foreword

Risk management is one of the most difficult and challenging tasks confronting industrial nations today. Most hazardous technologies confer substantial benefits on society in the form of better health, increased productivity, and, in general, a higher quality of life. A socially acceptable risk management strategy has to consider both the positive and the negative impacts of technology. The balancing process, however, is controversial because technological risks and benefits are often intangible, and there is no agreement on the way they should be valued. Scientific uncertainty also contributes to controversies about risk. Science cannot predict rare events with any accuracy, and our ability to measure the risks of chronic or cumulative exposure to hazardous substances is still limited. In the absence of definite knowledge, expert opinions tend to be colored by personal values as well as professional judgment, leading to different assessments of the significance of particular risks. In the effort to manage risks, public authorities are thus drawn into mediating not only among competing economic and political interests, but also among conflicting technical interpretations informed by widely divergent views about pollution and nature, illness and death.

Risk management has been seen in the past largely as a problem of national policy-making. This monograph, however, examines risk management from a cross-national perspective, comparing the policies adopted by several Western democracies to control a particular technological hazard: the risk of developing cancer from exposure to man-made chemicals. The monograph focuses on the use of science in the process of risk management and has three major objectives. The first objective is to add to our relatively limited knowledge about the ways different societies analyze scientific information about risk and cope with problems of technical uncertainty and expert conflict; more specifically, to examine the impact of different institutional and procedural arrangements on the public evaluation of risk. The second objective is to look at the scientific and political controversies surrounding the development of formal risk assessment methodologies and at the impact of these debates on the regulation of formaldehyde, a suspected carcinogen. The third objective is to explore how different national governments have tried to reconcile democratic values with the need for expert decision-making about risk. The monograph suggests that patterns of interaction between experts and the lay public reflect fundamental features of a country's political culture.

The choice of a comparative framework for this study was motivated by both practical and scholarly considerations. At the practical level, a comparative study can provide helpful information to policy-makers seeking improvements in their own approaches to risk management. Although the experiences of any one country may not be directly relevant to another, comparative analysis can provide valuable insights into the reasons for policy failure in a given national setting. For example, cross-national comparisons provide a basis for determining which problems of implementation are avoidable and which are more or less necessary consequences of scientific uncertainty or political cleavage. At a more theoretical level, the monograph hopes to make a contribution both to the field of comparative politics, where technical decision-making has received undeservedly little scholarly attention in the past, and to literature in the sociology of science. By focusing on the way scientific knowledge is produced and validated in a particular policy context—risk management—the monograph adds to current work on the social construction of science.

This monograph is an outgrowth of two earlier collaborative projects in which I was fortunate enough to participate. I was initially drawn to the comparative study of risk management through a research project on chemical regulation in Europe and the United States carried out jointly with two colleagues, Ronald Brickman and Thomas Ilgen. A book resulting from that study, *Controlling Chemicals: The Politics of Regulation in Europe and the United States,* has been published by Cornell University Press. As a follow-up to that project, Ronald Brickman and I organized a small international conference in August 1983: "Scientific Information and Public Decision-Making on Toxic Chemicals: An International Comparison." The conference was attended by twenty-six participants from ten countries, including high-level national and international administrators, scientists, legal experts, interest group representatives, and academic social scientists. This monograph owes an enormous debt to the conference, both because the meeting generated new information about carcinogen control policies in several countries and because participants from different national and disciplinary backgrounds brought varied critical insights to bear on the problem of risk management. I am particularly indebted to the reports presented by five working groups on cross-national similarities and differences relating to the following topics: the identification and classification of carcinogens, the regulation of formaldehyde, the separation of science from policy, risk assessment, and mechanisms for developing consensus in the policy system.

The research leading to this monograph would not have been possible without the generous support of several different funding agencies. The National Science Foundation and the Volkswagen Foundation supported the study of chemical regulation in four countries. In addition, both Ronald Brickman and I received fellowships from the German Marshall Fund, which enabled us to carry that project to completion. The international conference was supported by travel grants from the National Science Foundation and the German Marshall Fund, as well as the Russell Sage Foundation. The Rockefeller Foundation provided invaluable assistance by making available its Bellagio Study and Conference Center for the meeting. Finally, follow-up grants from the German Marshall Fund and the Russell Sage Foundation gave me an opportunity to develop the present comparative study on the use of science in risk management. I would like to thank all these organizations for their support. A special word of thanks is due as well to the Rockefeller Foundation's staff in Bellagio, whose smooth handling of all logistical problems ensured the success of the international conference.

I am grateful to a number of friends and colleagues who read and commented on earlier versions of this monograph. In particular, I would like to thank Edward Burger, Cyril Burgess, Lennart Danielson, Stephen Hilgartner, Thomas Ilgen, Howard Kunreuther, Dorothy Nelkin, and Brian Wynne. Their discerning comments helped me greatly in refining and sharpening many of the points made in this monograph. I would also like to thank Ronald Brickman for many productive discussions about science policy and comparative politics during the planning stages of the Bellagio Conference. Finally, I would like to express my appreciation to Sandra Kisner for her able assistance in preparing the manuscript for publication.

Contents

Avoiding technological risks is a central preoccupation of our age. We are haunted daily by risks of varying probability, magnitude, and emotive impact: dioxin in the air, trihalomethanes in the drinking water, pesticides on our food, drunken drivers on the highways, nuclear power plants in our backyards, and overarching all, the threat of extinction through war. Toxic chemicals figure prominently in our images of disaster. Most technologically advanced countries have experienced their distinctive national trauma with toxic substances: chemical plant explosions in Italy and Great Britain, a calamitous gas leak in India, mercury poisoning in Japan, the slow death of the Black Forest in Germany, and the "ticking time bomb" of hazardous waste sites in the United States. Such catastrophes have helped push risk management to the forefront of our scientific, political, and public policy agendas. We expect our scientists to make increasingly sophisticated measurements of risk and our government officials to translate this information into immediate and effective policy prescriptions.

The use of science in risk management is the subject of this monograph. The topic has attracted considerable attention in recent years not only among policy-makers, but also among concerned interest groups, scientists, and academic "science-watchers." For policy-makers and the public, a prime challenge is to devise scientifically credible ways of dealing with technological risk, since information about such risks is usually incomplete and subject to differing interpretations. Regulatory policy often has to strike a balance between the benefits of waiting for definite scientific proof and the costs of exposing the public to risk until such proofs are available. Groups who are threatened by technology understandably want to make sure that their interests are adequately considered in this balancing process. However, designing effective participatory mechanisms for the lay public is increasingly difficult in a decision-making environment heavily dominated by technical expertise.

The scientific community has discovered that it, too, has much to gain from a closer familiarity with the procedures developed by political officials to mediate expert disagreements and to bridge uncertainties in the technical record. Scientists have a large stake in assuring that such procedures do not impede progress in science or compromise the norms of distinterestedness and objectivity which are universally regarded as hallmarks of good science. For academic observers of science, the analysis of science-based regulatory decisions offers insights into the nature of scientific uncertainty, the negotiation of competing scientific claims, and the institutional conflicts that arise between science and other societal interests when scientific information becomes a key factor in political decision-making.

Many risks of modern technological civilization, including those created by toxic chemicals, are global in origin and impact. It is difficult to imagine solutions to transboundary problems such as pesticide pollution, acid rain, or the "greenhouse effect" without cooperation among the scientific, regulatory, and business communities of many different countries. Although these risks are transnational in character, surprisingly little comparative research has been done on the way different societies think about and seek to control them. The dearth of cross-national research can be attributed, in part, to the provincialism of traditional policy analysis. Such studies tend to regard risk management decisions as the product of distinctively national legal and administrative processes and are skeptical about the possibility that lessons learned within one policy system can be transferred to another.

Accordingly, studies of risk management by policy analysts have usually focused on the experiences of single nations.

Belief in the universality of science is another major factor that discourages comparative research on risk. When science is viewed as the primary determinant of risk management policy, the possibility of cross-cultural variation in the analysis and control of risk tends to be downplayed. Yet a growing body of literature in the sociology and anthropology of science challenges the notion of scientific determinism and emphasizes the role of cultural factors in shaping public responses to risk. Faith in science's independence from social influences has gradually eroded under the scrutiny of a generation of sociologists led by such influential figures as Robert Merton[1] and Thomas Kuhn.[2] Among studies focusing specifically on risk, Mary Douglas's work is especially notable for showing intricate connections between beliefs about pollution and other social concerns in both primitive and advanced societies.[3] A number of scholars have used the framework of decision theory developed by Fischhoff, Slovic, and Lichtenstein to demonstrate how ideological and cultural factors influence public perceptions of risk.[4] This research both documents and partly explains the differences that are frequently found between "lay" and "expert" assessments of risk. The political alignments that underlie modern scientific controversies have been explored in detail by Dorothy Nelkin and others interested in the politics of technical decisions.[5]

These lines of research all suggest that comparative analysis can offer special insights into the problems of using science in technological risk management. Studies across several countries can illuminate the ways in which particular legal and institutional features color the interpretation of scientific data and influence the resolution of technical controversies. Such comparisons make it possible to identify the strengths and weaknesses of alternative national approaches to dealing with expert conflicts. In this way, cross-national research advances both the descriptive analysis of risk management and the prescriptive goal of improving existing mechanisms of scientific decision-making. More generally, understanding the role of cultural factors in the assessment and management of risk promotes a more sophisticated appraisal of the limits of science as a tool for public policy-making about risk.

Within the last decade, a handful of scholars from a variety of disciplines have begun making explicit comparisons among the risk management policies of different technologically advanced countries. Though all of these studies fall under the broad heading of policy research, they are distinguished by different methodological approaches and they display different levels of interest in the scientific basis for risk management decisions.

One approach has been to investigate risk management primarily within the framework of comparative politics. Such studies include Lundqvist's work on clean air policies in Sweden and the United States,[6] Nelkin and Pollak's comparison of the French and German anti-nuclear movements,[7] and Kelman's analysis of Swedish and American occupational safety and health policy.[8] In a related vein, Kunreuther, Linnerooth, and Starnes's volume on the siting of liquefied natural gas facilities in Europe and the United States examines the impact of different institutional arrangements on the analysis and management of risk.[9] Other scholars are concerned with risk management primarily as an indicator of national regulatory styles and the structure of business-government relations. For example, Vogel's work on British and American environmental policies[10] and Badaracco's case study of vinyl chloride regulation in four countries[11] both draw contrasts between the essentially "cooperative" European approach to risk management and the more "confrontational" approach prevailing in the United States. Scientific issues and the role of the scientific community have played at best a peripheral role in these studies, which focus rather on the demands of interest groups and the responsiveness of political institutions to claims about risk. For purposes of cross-national comparison, science is held to be a constant, and relatively little attention is devoted to the activities of scientific elites or to variations in the use of technical information by private pressure groups.

A quite different orientation to the comparative study of risk management has emerged from the tradition of critical studies in science. A central assumption in this body of work is that science itself is not immune to social and cultural pressures; to varying degrees, scientific knowledge is "socially constructed." Sociologists of science have found support for this hypothesis in comparative research, particularly in the discovery that the same risk has been assessed differently by regulators and their scientific advisers in different national settings. Thus, both a study of pesticide regulation by Gillespie, Eva, and Johnston[12] and a study of the estrogen replacement controversy by McCrea and Markle[13] asked why British and American advisory committees, acting on the basis of the same technical record, reached different conclusions about risk. Their work sought explanations in a variety of institutional variables ranging from the internal organization of the relevant administrative agencies to the ideological concerns of scientists and affected interest groups.

One of the few attempts to marry the sociology of science perspective with the comparative politics approach was undertaken in a four-country comparison of chemical control policies by Brickman, Jasanoff, and Ilgen.[14] To test the impact of politics on science, this study systematically investigated the positions adopted by scientists, interest groups, and government officials in Europe and the United States with respect to the identification and control of carcinogens. One conclusion of the book was that a fundamental feature of political organization—the allocation of political authority among the three branches of government— heavily influences the form and intensity of scientific debates relating to risk. In particular, the extreme fragmentation of political power in the United States not only increases the demand for scientific explanations of risk decisions, but also encourages competition among different perceptions of risk. This helps explain why the technical basis for regulation is debated more extensively and at a higher level of sophistication in the United States than in Britain, France, or West Germany.

This monograph builds on the existing comparative literature on risk management and seeks to extend it in three ways. First, it explores some of the special institutional and procedural problems occasioned by the use of scientific information in risk management. One problem arises from the fact that decisions about risk are neither wholly scientific nor wholly political, and therefore demand novel collaborations between scientists, public officials, and private interest groups. Weinberg's seminal work on science and transscience called attention to the fact that many issues relevant to risk management lie outside the bounds of scientific investigation. In Weinberg's words, such questions "may arise in or around science, and can be stated in the language of science, [but] they are unanswerable by science—that is, they transcend science."[15] Cross-national analysis helps define the boundaries between the scientific and transscientific aspects of risk management and illustrates the methods that policy-makers can adopt in dealing with issues at the borderline of science and politics.

5

Another problem—the need to secure dependable or "certified" knowledge—is common to all consumers of science, whether they are scientists or government agencies. In the context of risk management, however, the problem of quality control acquires a special edge, because the science available to policy-makers is new or contested and because political officials generally cannot afford to wait for the gradual processes of scientific dissemination to sift good studies and methodologies from bad. A comparative study of risk management can provide useful information about the procedures that governmental agencies can use to control the quality of policy-relevant science.

Second, the monograph compares emerging national policies concerning the use of quantitative risk assessment in the regulation of hazardous technologies, particularly toxic chemicals. Although many observers believe that such methodologies will play an increasingly important role in worldwide efforts to manage technological risks, the scientific and political conflicts surrounding risk assessment have not yet been extensively studied in a cross-national framework. The current governmental interest in risk assessment developed largely as a result of attempts by the United States and other industrial countries to regulate certain low-probability threats to public health, including those presented by radiation and by chemicals suspected of causing cancer. This monograph examines the history of carcinogen regulation in Europe and North America during the 1970s in order to explain some of the differences in current national preferences for the use of quantitative risk assessment.

Third, this monograph uses comparative analysis to enlarge our understanding of the way political cultures influence the balance of power between citizens and technical elites in modern democracies.

As we approach the end of the twentieth century, we appear to have unleashed a variety of technologies that threaten not only our immediate health, safety, and well-being, but the continued survival of humanity. In seeking to master these pervasive risks, democratic societies are committed to preserving certain basic values, such as the citizen's right to understand and to participate in governmental decision-making. In this context, the relationship between the average citizen and the expert who possesses specialized knowledge about risk has become a matter of acute concern. With science and technology playing an ever more important role in risk management, how can private citizens strike a reasonable balance between activism and restraint, between deference and skepticism, in their relations with technical experts? Are we moving, as Dickson contends,[16] into an era of dangerous complacency about rule by technocrats? To what extent do national political cultures condition the relationship between experts and the lay public in the policy process? The existing scholarship on comparative political culture has largely neglected these special problems of democracy in a technological age.[17]

In exploring these broad issues of science policy and politics, the monograph focuses on a specific area of risk management: the regulation of chemical carcinogens. Carcinogens as a class have aroused greater public concern and attracted more regulatory attention in the past two decades than most other categories of toxic substances. As a result, both the scientific and policy issues relevant to the management of carcinogenic risk have been widely debated in public, creating a useful record for comparative analysis. Examples of divergent national approaches to the regulation of carcinogens are drawn from the United States, Canada, and several European countries. In all of these countries, a relatively open decision-making system makes it possible to retrieve information about major policy initiatives and to trace the history of particular regulatory decisions. There are numerous reasons to expect a parallel development of risk management policies in all the countries discussed in this monograph. They have broadly similar political systems, share a common scientific tradition, and participate in joint decision-making and information exchange through such international organizations as the United Nations and the Organisation for Economic Cooperation and Development. Divergences among them are thus particularly intriguing and provide a rich basis for studying the problems and limitations of alternative national policies for the assessment and control of risk.

The succeeding chapters begin with specific issues of carcinogenic risk management and move to larger questions about science policy and political culture. Chapters 2–5 present some basic contrasts among national approaches to controlling carcinogenic risk. An overview of "cancer policies" in several countries in chapter 2 is followed by an analysis in chapters 3 and 4 of national procedures for identifying carcinogens and quantitatively estimating their risks. Chapter 5 discusses the response of policy systems to advances in knowledge about the mechanisms of cancer causation. Chapter 6 looks at the impact of national philosophies of risk management on the regulation of formaldehyde, a suspected human carcinogen. The next two chapters examine the institutional choices made by different governments for managing scientific and political disputes about risk. Specifically, chapter 7 focuses on institutional arrangements for public participation and relates these to underlying features of each country's political culture. Chapter 8 examines the role that two relatively neutral sources of expertise—the scientific community and international organizations—can expect to play in resolving controversies about regulatory science. The concluding chapter summarizes the major findings of the comparative study and indicates some directions for future research.

Cancer is not only one of the leading causes of death in industrial societies, but a disease that inspires particular terror. Its unpredictability, frequent irreversibility, and long latency have invested cancer with the special symbolic resonance described by Susan Sontag in *Illness as Metaphor*.[18] For many, the name of the disease remains taboo. Kipling said in 1924, in a powerful story about obsession and loss, "Human nature seldom walks up to the word 'cancer.' "[19]

Nearly half a century has passed since Auden wrote of cancer:

> Nobody knows what the cause is
>   Though some pretend they do;
> It's like some hidden assassin
>   Waiting to strike at you.[20]

In spite of countless scientific advances in the intervening years, the precise "cause" of cancer still eludes us in most cases, and the dread expressed in Auden's poem is still the dominant feeling associated with the disease. This no doubt explains why governmental and even industrial organizations in many Western countries now agree that regulators are right to treat the risks presented by carcinogens with special sensitivity. Yet the assumptions and methods that guide the regulation of carcinogens vary bewilderingly not only from one country to another, but also among regulatory programs within the same country. Though cancer may be the universal enemy, the urge to wage war on chemical carcinogens seems very unevenly developed among public regulatory authorities.

The term "cancer policy" was coined in the United States in the 1970s to describe the special principles used by administrative agencies and scientific advisory bodies in identifying carcinogens and assessing their risks. The use of this term is symptomatic of the striking emphasis on carcinogens that has distinguished U.S. regulatory policy in the past fifteen years. Numerous studies have documented the intense legal and political pressures that impelled U.S. agencies to expand their research programs on carcinogens, and, more recently, to adopt systematic policies for evaluating the scientific evidence used in regulating carcinogens.[21]

The most distinctive feature of the cancer policies developed in the United States is their assumption that gaps between science and policy should be bridged by means of administrative rules. Formal statements about how to test carcinogens and interpret these tests proceed from a belief that, when all the scientific evidence is in, regulators will still be confronted by numerous uncertainties and expert conflicts. Science alone will not be sufficient to dictate the correct policy choice. In order to make policy in a publicly accountable manner, regulators should therefore state principled rules for overcoming the expected omissions and conflicts in the scientific record.

One of the most comprehensive U.S. cancer policies was promulgated by the Occupational Safety and Health Administration (OSHA) in 1980.[22] It sought to establish a framework of rules that would encompass every significant uncertainty in the regulatory process. Wherever the scientific evidence could point to more than one inference, OSHA provided a rule to guide the decision-maker in a specified direction. OSHA's guiding philosophy was to require that the most conservative, scientifically tenable assumption (that is, the one most likely to increase the number of substances identified as carcinogens) should be used in selecting among multiple inferences.[23]

Another distinguishing feature of U.S. cancer policies promulgated in the 1970s was their assumption that carcinogens should be regulated to the lowest technologically feasible limit. This philosophy was initially founded on a scientific rationale. The dominant opinion among U.S. cancer experts has long been that it is either impossible or impractical to find a "threshold" below which individuals can safely be exposed to carcinogens. Until quite recently, this meant that regulators had only two practical alternatives to follow in the interests of public safety: either to ban all exposure to carcinogens, thereby reducing the risk of chemically induced cancer to zero, or to restrict such exposures as far as humanly possible. A controversial legislative endorsement of the zero-risk approach is enshrined in the Delaney clause of the Federal Food, Drug, and Cosmetic Act,[24] which forbids the introduction of most carcinogenic additives into food. The economic impracticability of this approach was soon recognized, but throughout the 1970s the spirit of the Delaney clause enjoyed broad popular support and continued to guide U.S. lawmakers, administrators, and the courts.[25] As a result, a working consensus developed around the proposition that the most stringent regulatory standards should be used in controlling substances shown to cause cancer in humans or animals.

Much of the controversy surrounding carcinogen regulation in the 1980s reflects a wearing away of that social consensus under the combined pressure of economics, a changing public attitude to governmental intervention, and scientific advances that call into question the "no threshold" assumption about carcinogens. In particular, both governmental agencies and the public are now more sympathetic to the view that all animal carcinogens do not present equivalent risks to humans. U.S. policy-makers have accordingly shifted their attention to devising systematic principles for assessing the relative risks of different carcinogenic compounds. These initiatives, however, reflect the same preference for explicit decision-making rules that guided the development of the earlier cancer policies (see chapter 5).

Attempts to develop cancer policies have been incomparably less systematic and deliberate in Europe and Canada than in the United States. The governing "policy" is sometimes nothing more than an admission that the fear of cancer justifies separate legislative treatment for carcinogens, particularly in the occupational environment. The need for special risk assessment procedures or safety goals, however, is explicitly denied by some industrial and governmental organizations. For example, both the European Council of Chemical Manufacturers' Federations and the European Chemical Industry Ecology and Toxicology Centre have endorsed the concept of separate legislation, but have emphasized that the regulation of carcinogens should rest on the same general principles of risk assessment as are used for other toxic substances.[26] One influential regulatory agency, Britain's Health and Safety Executive (HSE), agrees with these associations in favoring an "integrated" approach to regulating carcinogens and other hazardous substances.[27]

By contrast, British labor organizations have urged their government to adopt a cancer policy based not merely on separate legislation, but also on a regulatory philosophy that takes into account the special human aversion to carcinogenic risk. Thus, the Association of Scientific, Technical and Managerial Staffs, Britain's leading white-collar union, recommended in 1980 that a number of specialized measures be used in controlling carcinogens, including the screening of all commercially used materials for carcinogenicity, a clear labeling scheme, comprehensive record-keeping, and control of identified carcinogens to the lowest feasible level of exposure.[28] Some of these recommendations have by now been officially accepted, though notably not in the form of an explicit cancer policy. For example, the Notification of New Substances Regulations requires screening of new chemicals for carcinogenicity, and labeling of carcinogens is required by the Classification, Packaging and Labelling Regulation of 1984. Both sets of regulations were issued under authority of the Health and Safety at Work Act (HSW Act) of 1974. Unlike the U.S. cancer policies, however, these requirements do not add up to a comprehensive strategy for regulating *all* carcinogens in the workplace and thus fall short of meeting labor's demand for systematic control of these substances.

A Royal Society study group report concluded in 1983 that British regulatory strategy for ionizing radiation and some carcinogens is based on a recognition that these substances "are useful, . . . have no substitutes that are demonstrably less harmful, and have no observable safe thresholds."[29] The report suggests that regulation of such substances should be based on a balancing of risks and benefits and should incorporate the following goals:

(a) an upper limit of risk which should not be exceeded for any individual;

(b) further control so far as is reasonably practicable, making allowance, if possible, for aversions to the higher levels of risk or detriment; and

(c) a cut-off in the deployment of resources below some level of exposure or detriment judged to be trivial.

British agencies, however, have refrained from making any such general statements about their goals and strategies in regulating carcinogenic risks. In fact, HSE officials view the third goal proposed by the Royal Society study group as problematic, since there are wide differences of opinion on what constitutes a "trivial" level of exposure to carcinogens.

Like Britain, France has never articulated any formal policies for regulating carcinogens in the workplace or the general environment. There are rare indications, especially in the area of occupational safety and health policy, that carcinogens are viewed with special concern. For example, experts working for the French government have acknowledged that safe thresholds of exposure cannot be established for such substances.[30] This recognition has led French authorities to employ medical monitoring and industrial hygiene requirements, rather than standard-setting, as the preferred means of protecting workers against occupational cancer. The list of diseases for which French workers are legally entitled to compensation includes a handful caused by exposure to carcinogens.[31] This, however, is standard practice in virtually every industrial country and does not betoken special sensitivity to carcinogens. Overall, it is fair to say that French attempts to control toxic chemicals have not yielded any package of policies aimed exclusively at carcinogens.

In several European countries, the formulation of a regulatory cancer policy begins with a listing of substances that present a risk of cancer to humans or animals. Such lists are usually developed in connection with governmental efforts to protect worker health. For example, in Finland occupational exposure to carcinogens is controlled pursuant to a governmental decision based on the Act of Safety at Work.[32] The core of the Finnish scheme is a register, maintained since 1979, listing carcinogens found in the workplace and recording all workers with definite, probable, or possible exposure to these substances. The register thus far lists only "established" human and animal carcinogens. Listing, in turn, triggers a variety of employer obligations, including record-keeping, medically monitoring exposed workers, and educating them about risks and how to avoid them. These extra duties reflect official acceptance of the fact that carcinogenic exposures should be viewed differently from other toxic exposures. The Finnish government, however, has not adopted the premise that carcinogens in the workplace should automatically be subject to more stringent engineering controls than other toxic agents. In fact, carcinogens requiring registration are divided into three categories corresponding to differing degrees of legal control.

In the Federal Republic of Germany, responsibility for controlling carcinogens is divided among several governmental and non-governmental organizations. The scientific basis for regulation is supplied by a commission of the Deutsche Forschungsgemeinschaft (DFG), which annually publishes a list of carcinogens grouped into three risk categories: human carcinogens, animal carcinogens, and substances presenting positive indications of carcinogenicity, but not definitely recognized as carcinogens. An expert committee of the Ministry of Labor establishes exposure standards for substances in the top two risk categories in accordance with the principle that exposures should be reduced to the lowest levels economically and technically feasible. The numerical exposure limits for carcinogens, known as "technical guiding concentrations" (TRKs), are supplemented by additional obligations for employers and employees, such as ventilation, medical supervision, or wearing of protective clothing, which are deemed necessary by the corporation that insures the chemical industry.[33]

In its approach to managing carcinogenic risk, Canada follows Britain and France rather than Finland or West Germany. The absence of a well-articulated Canadian policy for controlling carcinogens is in part a function of the way power is divided between the federal and provincial governments. In particular, occupational safety and health issues, including standard-setting, come mainly under provincial jurisdiction. As a result, there has been no occasion for federal authorities to develop a master list of carcinogens in the workplace or to consider a unified policy for reducing exposure to such substances. Beyond this, Canadian decision-making on toxic chemicals has followed the decentralized and consultative European model.[34] With limited resources for testing and evaluation, governmental departments have addressed the issue of carcinogenic risk on a case-by-case basis. Assessments within any agency are governed by its particular priorities and mission and are further influenced by agency-specific traditions of consulting with expert advisory committees, interest groups, and other governmental bodies. No single agency has powers comparable to those of the Environmental Protection Agency or OSHA. In a framework of multiple agencies with limited regulatory objectives, there has been understandably little support for a general cancer policy along lines proposed in the United States.

As these examples indicate, the variation among national cancer policies is considerable. Regulatory systems vary in the extent to which they acknowledge the need for separate legislative treatment of carcinogens, in their commitment to particular levels of risk reduction, and in their legal and institutional arrangements for controlling exposure. In France and Canada, it hardly makes sense to speak of an official cancer policy. In Britain, issues concerning carcinogens have achieved political prominence through labor's activities, but have not elicited a systematic policy response. Germany and Finland both have the rudiments of a cancer policy, though limited to the context of worker protection.

The policies of these countries, however, differ from those of the United States in one notable respect. Only in the United States have governmental agencies or their scientific advisers attempted to articulate their principles for dealing with uncertainty or incompleteness in the scientific evidence of carcinogenicity. For example, though Finnish officials and German scientists may have rigorous and systematic reasons for classifying carcinogens in different risk categories, they have not endeavored to make these reasons public. Nor have any European governments stated in general terms how stringently substances identified as carcinogens should be regulated. In the absence of a general policy for managing carcinogenic risk, controversial issues, such as how to interpret contradictory studies, have been decided in most countries on a case-by-case basis. Such decisions are generally made by expert committees, whose deliberations are usually confidential. As a result, there is no clear record of the principles of scientific interpretation used in individual cases or of changes in these principles over time.

In the United States, by contrast, regulators have undertaken to point out where, in their view, policy judgments have to supplement scientific evaluation. They have presumed, moreover, that such policies can be expressed in the form of general guidelines or rules which should be made available to the public. The effect of this strategy is to make the regulator's reasons for finding that substances present (or do not present) a carcinogenic hazard open and accessible to all. Any weaknesses in the scientific argument, as well as any substantial shifts from prior administrative policy, thus become relatively easy to detect. It is hardly surprising, therefore, that the federal government's cancer policies have aroused controversies such as those described in the following chapters.

In its simplest dictionary meaning, a carcinogen is a cancer-causing substance or, in slightly more technical language, anything that increases the incidence of neoplasms in *some* species. National regulatory agencies, however, are most concerned with carcinogens when there is reason to believe that they may cause cancer in humans. For the vast majority of potential carcinogens, the scientific basis for determining whether they will increase the incidence of human cancer is highly uncertain. Because of this uncertainty, labeling a substance as a "carcinogen" for regulatory purposes almost always involves a hypothetical exercise. The question regulators must ask is not "*Does* this substance cause cancer in humans?" but "Should this substance be treated *as if* it causes cancer in humans?" In most regulatory systems, governmental officials have considerable freedom to decide under what conditions they will treat a suspected carcinogen as a real human carcinogen. These criteria constitute a crucial element in each country's cancer policy. By defining and redefining them, regulators, like Humpty Dumpty in the looking-glass world, can make the term "carcinogen" mean just what they choose it to mean.

17

A comparison of carcinogen identification processes across several national and international agencies shows that there is considerable variation in the criteria used to decide whether a substance should be viewed as causing cancer in humans. National and international practices also vary with respect to articulating the reasons for designating possible carcinogens as actual carcinogens. Responsibility for developing and applying the principles of carcinogen identification is allocated differently among scientists and regulators in different countries. Finally, the extent of public debate over the identification of carcinogens has varied markedly across national boundaries.

Among the lists of carcinogens commonly used by regulators, those prepared by the International Agency for Research on Cancer (IARC), a branch of the World Health Organization, have attracted widest support from scientists, governmental officials, and private interest groups. Since 1971, IARC has published a series of monographs evaluating the carcinogenic risk of chemicals to humans. The principles and definitions used by IARC are regarded as authoritative by most governmental agencies. An important example is IARC's definition of "chemical carcinogenesis" as "the induction by chemicals of neoplasms that are not usually observed, the earlier induction by chemicals of neoplasms that are commonly observed, and/or the induction by chemicals of more neoplasms than are usually found."[35]

In its evaluations of particular chemicals IARC avoids the simple label "carcinogen." Instead, the agency makes separate findings with respect to animal and human carcinogenicity and assesses the weight of the evidence supporting each finding. IARC's expert working groups independently evaluate human epidemiological studies and animal data to determine whether either type of evidence is "sufficient," "limited," or "inadequate" for a finding of carcinogenicity, or whether there is "no evidence." While there is nothing absolute about these evidentiary standards, their use reflects the prevailing consensus among scientists affiliated with IARC. For example, IARC regards the evidence of carcinogenicity in animals as "sufficient" only when studies show "an increased incidence of malignant tumours: (i) in multiple species or strains, and/or (ii) in multiple experiments (routes and/or doses), and/or (iii) to an unusual degree (with regard to incidence, site, type and/or precocity of onset)." This definition means that if a substance meets the stated criteria, most cancer experts working through IARC are prepared to accept it as an animal carcinogen.

Inevitably, there is an element of discretion in applying these criteria to specific cases, particularly when judgments must be made on the basis of contradictory studies or when the significance of observed abnormalities is in doubt. For example, there are no hard and fast rules for deciding what to do when the data from two animal species do not agree, or when the only evidence of carcinogenicity is at an unreliable site such as the mouse liver. Nevertheless, most IARC experts would argue that the judgment required in making such decisions is merely ordinary scientific judgment. The IARC monographs attempt nothing more than to represent a scientific consensus about such issues. The agency's decisions to evaluate animal and human data separately, to assess only the weight of the evidence for each heading, and to formulate its conclusions in qualitative rather than quantitative terms are all consistent with this limited objective.

IARC expert groups enjoy one luxury that is not shared by their colleagues in national regulatory agencies or on governmental advisory committees. Since their activities do not entail automatic regulatory consequences, scientists working for IARC need not concern themselves with the potential economic or political impact of their decisions. By contrast, when carcinogen evaluation takes place within a regulatory environment, significant costs and risks hang upon the final determination. The costs of choosing the wrong interpretation, in particular, can be enormous, whether the error is in the direction of overestimating or underestimating the actual level of risk. Legal considerations as well impinge on the evaluation of carcinogens at the national level, since some legislative frameworks require carcinogens to be regulated more stringently than other toxic substances. These factors help explain why governmental agencies in the major chemical-producing nations have been reluctant to base their regulatory decisions purely upon IARC's scheme for identifying and classifying carcinogens.

The classification scheme used by the Deutsche Forschungsgemeinschaft (DFG) commission on workplace hazards in Germany parallels the IARC system in separately listing the substances that pose a risk to humans (Group A1) and those that are known to cause cancer only in animals (Group A2).[36] A third grouping, consisting of compounds "justifiably suspected of having carcinogenic potential" (Group B), seems roughly to correspond to IARC's limited evidence category. Unlike the IARC evaluations, however, the lists developed by the DFG commission are directly incorporated into a governmental decision-making process that assigns different regulatory consequences to chemicals in the three categories. For substances in Group A, for example, employers are required to undertake stringent monitoring of exposure levels and biological monitoring of exposed workers.[37] More important, the DFG commission acknowledges that no safe level of exposure can be established for these substances on the basis of available animal or epidemiological studies. Hence, the presumption is that workers can be adequately protected against substances in Group A only if exposure is reduced to the limits of economic and technical feasibility. For substances in Group B, however, the DFG commission prescribes so-called MAK-values, or maximum allowable levels of exposure, which are considered "safe." There is no expectation that these standards should be progressively reduced to the extent that technology permits. Moreover, for Group B substances, employers are not subject to the strict handling and monitoring requirements demanded for substances in Group A. In effect, then, only the substances in Groups A1 and A2 are treated *as if* they are high-risk human carcinogens, and there is a tacit understanding among all concerned parties that exceptional regulatory costs are warranted in preventing exposure to these chemicals.

West Germany's occupational "cancer policy" incorporates a clear strategic decision: that a carcinogenic risk of serious regulatory concern will be presumed to exist not only where there is epidemiological evidence of cancer-causation, but also when there is unmistakable evidence of carcinogenicity from animal experimentation. Yet the organization of the regulatory process conceals rather than clarifies this important policy choice. Institutionally, the process of scientific decision-making (listing by the DFG commission) is separated from the phase of political decision-making (standard-setting by the Labor Ministry's advisory committee). The critical linkages between these two activities are not spelled out in any official policy document, but have evolved informally over time and are known only to participants in the process. Moreover, the principal decision-making bodies are unconnected by formal institutional or professional ties: the one is an autonomous scientific organization, operating according to its own rules of procedure and professional responsibility; the other is an official advisory body, appointed in accordance with legal requirements, and charged with providing technical guidance to the government on a whole range of policy issues. There is no hard evidence indicating that either group influences the actions of the other. If any political influence is exercised on the scientific evaluation process, it is done *sub silentio,* with no documentary record prepared for public edification.[38]

In contrast to German policy, which has accorded a special status to occupational carcinogens, the British regulatory system has avoided recognizing carcinogenicity as a trigger for heightened official concern. Since the Carcinogenic Substances Regulations of 1967, which essentially prohibited the manufacture of chemicals in the benzidine dye family, Britain has not promulgated any regulation specifically directed at carcinogens. Official policy continues to treat carcinogens like any other toxic substances. Since no British agency maintains lists of carcinogens, it is difficult to determine how narrowly regulators define this class of substances. The effort to find systematic patterns in British carcinogen regulation is further complicated by the fact that scientific advisory committees do not routinely publish their findings. As a result, the information available about particular chemical control decisions is ad hoc and fragmentary. However, a few comparative studies of British and American regulation suggest that British officials are reluctant to recognize any substance as carcinogenic unless there is some corroborating human epidemiological evidence.[39]

It is hard to imagine a sharper contrast to the situation in the United States. Since the mid-1970s, the Environmental Protection Agency (EPA), the Occupational Safety and Health Administration (OSHA), and the Interagency Regulatory Liaison Group, an interdepartmental body active during the Carter Administration,[40] have all been involved in developing workable policies for identifying carcinogens and assessing their risks. Guidelines for testing carcinogens and evaluating experimental data have also emerged from the National Cancer Institute and, more recently, from the President's Office of Science and Technology Policy.[41] The key regulatory agencies have acknowledged quite explicitly that the class of substances to be treated as carcinogens for purposes of regulation should be larger than the class of substances known to cause cancer in humans. Their institutional energies have been devoted to the task of articulating as precisely as possible what substances other than known human carcinogens should properly be included in the broader class of "regulatory carcinogens." These efforts, in turn, have provoked a series of controversies at the borderline of science and policy for which there are no real parallels in other advanced industrial countries.

Controversies about the identification of carcinogens in the United States have been thoroughly documented in the policy literature. As mentioned earlier, these debates centered primarily on attempts by EPA and OSHA to develop generic principles for identifying substances presenting enough risk of cancer to merit stringent regulation. Both U.S. agencies adopted positions that must be considered radical compared with initiatives in other countries. For example, OSHA's cancer policy provided that positive evidence from even a single well-conducted animal study should outweigh nonpositive data from epidemiological surveys and that a substance could be classified as a high-risk carcinogen on the basis of positive bioassay results regardless of the dosage at which cancer was induced in the experimental animals.[42]

Systematic implementation of such policies would have led to the designation of many more chemicals as high-risk carcinogens than under any other national or international classification scheme. Moreover, OSHA interpreted its enabling statute to mean that all these substances could then be regulated to the limit of economic and technological feasibility. The agency officials who developed the cancer policy deny that these draconian implications would ever have been realized in practice. The agency's own legal staff estimated that the policy would enable OSHA to speed up its activities from one or two rule-making proceedings per year to at most a dozen.[43] The chemical industry, however, was not prepared to live with even these cautious predictions. Deeply concerned about the potential impact of the cancer policy, industry came forward with a host of arguments challenging both the legality of the generic approach and the scientific validity of particular decision-making principles, such as OSHA's uncritical acceptance of data from high-dose animal tests.

The official response to these challenges during the first Reagan term was to retreat from some of the most far-reaching principles endorsed by the previous administration. OSHA's cancer policy was suspended, while EPA made efforts to abandon one of its central doctrines: that it is appropriate to classify substances as presenting a serious carcinogenic risk to humans solely on the basis of positive animal studies. EPA did not openly disavow this doctrine, but instead advanced new reasons for discriminating more carefully among substances shown to cause cancer in animals. Agency officials argued in a series of internal policy memoranda that carcinogens showing no evidence of genotoxicity (designated as "epigenetic" carcinogens) could safely be placed in a lower risk category and regulated on the same basis as noncarcinogenic compounds.[44] For such substances, EPA seemed to be moving toward the position that it was possible to establish a safe threshold of exposure, although thresholds were still ruled out for genotoxic compounds.

When the agency's internal deliberations became public, knowledgeable outsiders quickly recognized that EPA's real objective was to change its working definition of a carcinogen. Instead of classifying all known animal carcinogens in the highest risk category, EPA now wanted to limit this classification to a smaller subgroup consisting only of genotoxic animal carcinogens. In the ensuing public furor, a number of eminent scientists came forward to testify that there was no basis in science for the distinction EPA was seeking to draw between genotoxic and nongenotoxic compounds.[45] These external peer reviewers denounced EPA's proposed policies as a pseudo-scientific ploy designed to conceal a major policy shift toward less stringent regulation. Unable to give scientific content to the concept of an "epigenetic" compound, EPA quietly dropped the term from its carcinogen assessment vocabulary.

For complex reasons, this kind of open conflict between scientists and regulatory agencies seldom surfaces in other Western democracies. As the comparison of national cancer identification policies indicates, American administrators assume broader powers than their European counterparts in deciding questions that lie close to the boundaries of established science. In Europe, scientists are often the effective policy-makers, since a recommendation by a scientific panel tends to decide the ultimate policy outcome. In the United States, the situation almost seems reversed. Issues which European agencies would unhesitatingly delegate to their scientific advisers are frequently resolved in the United States as "policy" issues by politically appointed administrators. A good example is OSHA's decision to spell out in its cancer policy the criteria by which certain categories of evidence, such as nonpositive epidemiological studies, would be judged acceptable or unacceptable.[46]

At the same time, the American penchant for making risk management policy in a public arena generates strong pressures for regulators to seek rational, seemingly apolitical justifications for difficult decisions or shifts in strategy. Agencies therefore attempt wherever possible to clothe their risk decisions in scientific terms. The genotoxicity debate and its outcome show how such a process can backfire. The U.S. scientific community may be prepared to grant the agencies control over decisions in which science and policy are intermingled, but there is a fundamental instability in this division of power. Scientists are always suspicious that, under the guise of making science policy decisions, administrative agencies will manipulate scientific information for political ends or otherwise make decisions that are contrary to good science. As a result, independent scientists are prepared to review agency determinations and to offer public criticism at the invitation of Congress or concerned private interest groups.

In the U.S. context, then, vigorous policing of the regulatory agencies by the scientific establishment seems unavoidable and generally serves as a useful check on broad agency control over issues at the borderline of science and policy. The need for such supervision is vastly reduced in countries where the resolution of most science policy issues is entrusted to the scientific community from the start.

Perhaps the most dramatic shift in U.S. policy on carcinogens in this decade has been the acceptance of quantitative risk assessment as an indispensable analytical instrument for regulatory decision-making. Before 1980, the agencies concerned with regulating carcinogens took a cautious approach to quantifying risk. The position adopted by the Interagency Regulatory Liaison Group (IRLG) in its 1979 guidelines, for example, was that quantitative assessments of cancer risks should be used only in establishing priorities and for purposes of obtaining very rough estimates of the magnitude of risk.[47] The Occupational Safety and Health Administration (OSHA) expressed an even more skeptical attitude not only in its cancer policy,[48] but in failing to perform a quantitative risk assessment for the benzene exposure standard promulgated in 1978. Quite simply, OSHA refused to acknowledge that risk assessment was an essential step in standard-setting under the Occupational Safety and Health Act.

Two developments, one originating in the Supreme Court and the other in the National Academy of Sciences (NAS), signaled changes in this official orientation to risk assessment. In 1980, the Supreme Court invalidated OSHA's new benzene standard, although it was established in accordance with the general principles laid out in the cancer policy.[49] The Court asked the agency to demonstrate, by means of appropriate quantitative methods, that there was a significant risk to workers at the existing exposure standard and that this risk could be reduced by lowering the exposure level tenfold.

In 1983, NAS published a report calling upon the federal government to make a clearer separation between the scientific and political phases of risk management.[50] Agencies were asked to distinguish between an objective, quantitative approach to determining risk (assessment) and a subjective, political approach to developing regulatory controls (management). The proposal reflected the thinking of prominent agency officials and science advisers, some of whom were members of the NAS committee. William Ruckelshaus, newly reappointed to head the Environmental Protection Agency (EPA), was an enthusiastic supporter of the bifurcated conceptual scheme proposed by NAS.[51] Ruckelshaus agreed that separating "risk assessment" from "risk management" would improve EPA's credibility by clarifying the scientific basis for the agency's policy choices. Scientists, too, generally viewed the NAS proposal as a useful way to insulate the scientific phase of risk management from manipulation by politically motivated agency officials.

Rule-making practices in some agencies changed almost overnight in response to these events. OSHA, the agency most directly affected by the Supreme Court's benzene ruling, began commissioning risk assessments for carcinogens on its regulatory agenda, including benzene and formaldehyde. The Consumer Product Safety Commission (CPSC) performed a quantitative risk assessment for urea-formaldehyde foam insulation (UFFI), which became the first commercially significant product to be regulated by CPSC on the strength of a statistical projection of cancer risks.[52] Unlike OSHA and CPSC, EPA was doing risk assessments for carcinogens in the late 1970s. But EPA, too, revised its guidelines on carcinogen risk assessment and more explicitly endorsed the use of quantitative "risk characterizations," though with a number of reservations and qualifications.[53]

With the appropriateness of risk assessment firmly established, debate within the regulatory agencies has moved on to narrower methodological issues. The qualitative interpretation of animal tests, often referred to as hazard identification, remains a recognized focus of controversy. For example, EPA is aware that it will continue to confront disputes about whether tumor data from different sites should be aggregated and whether benign as well as malignant tumors should be counted in plotting a dose-response curve. At the same time, a new center of controversy has developed around the selection of statistical models for high to low dose extrapolation, forcing agencies to deal with a different set of questions. Should linearity always be assumed at low doses? When is it proper to select a model on the basis of criteria other than "goodness of fit," that is, the closeness of the match between the observed data points and the predictive model? How should the uncertainties in the quantitative estimate be represented, and how can they be most effectively communicated to regulators and the public?[54]

While official discussion of risk assessment centers on technical questions like these, considerable doubt still remains about the advisability of relying on methods so fraught with uncertainty. Even guidelines favoring the concept of risk assessment, such as those recently published by EPA, emphasize the multiple sources of uncertainty in making numerical risk assessments. Less guarded skepticism has been voiced by individual agency officials, who compare risk assessment to anything from a "circumstantial murder trial" to "pulling numbers out of thin air."[55] Environmentalists, on the whole, are critical of risk assessment on the grounds that numbers create a false impression of certainty and may be used by regulators without proper regard for the imperfections of the underlying science.[56] Industry representatives, by contrast, frequently support the use of risk assessment in their public statements. But litigation over CPSC's ban on UFFI indicated that manufacturers are perfectly prepared to argue the opposite position when the results of quantitative analysis are harmful to their economic interests.[57]

One area of risk assessment where industry's interests can be expected to converge with those of regulatory agencies is the effort to develop a workable concept of *de minimis* risk, which is currently attracting considerable attention in the United States. The underlying idea is simple: there are some risks that are too small to be of societal concern, and if these negligible or *de minimis* risks can be identified, then scarce resources do not have to be spent in controlling them. The benzene case and a number of other judicial decisions provide legal support for the position that agencies should not attempt to regulate risks that are too small to merit public concern.[58] The problem, however, is to find an acceptable method of defining truly *de minimis* risks. Both EPA and FDA have developed guidelines suggesting that risks of 1 in 1 million should be treated as *de minimis* for regulatory purposes.[59] These efforts have not been widely publicized in the past, partly because they appear to place an upper limit on the value of human life, an exercise that U.S. critics of cost-benefit analysis have always regarded with particular disfavor.[60] A consensus is now emerging that *de minimis* risk levels should not be viewed as "acceptable," since this term raises the difficult political question, "Acceptable to whom?" Rather, the concept should be used primarily as a tool for establishing priorities, so that agencies do not try to regulate *de minimis* risks when larger risks have not been adequately addressed. In any event, recent studies of *de minimis* risk note that substantial methodological problems must be overcome before the concept finds noncontroversial applications in regulatory decision-making.[61]

In Europe and Canada, regulatory interest in risk assessment has been slower to develop and, consistent with a lower emphasis on carcinogens, methodological discussions focus less exclusively on techniques for predicting cancer risks. In Britain the term "risk assessment" has been applied to an entire array of methods for systematically evaluating and characterizing risk. For example, the Royal Society study group used the term to encompass two very different analytical processes: risk estimation and risk evaluation.[62] As defined by the Royal Society, risk estimation is the procedure that most closely approximates what U.S. regulators term risk assessment. Risk estimation includes both the identification of adverse effects and the evaluation of their magnitude and probability. Risk evaluation, by contrast, refers to the evaluation of the impact of risk on those affected; its components include studies of risk perception and risk-benefit analysis. In the U.S. decision-making context, such impact considerations enter, if at all, into the management rather than the assessment of risk.

Besides reviewing the risk assessment literature in detail, the Royal Society report provides some guidelines about using quantitative estimates of risk. For example, in discussing the upper limit of risk to an individual, the report suggests that an annual risk of death of 1 in 1,000 might not be "*totally* unacceptable provided that the individual at risk knew of the situation, judged he had some commensurate benefit as a result, and understood that everything reasonable had already been done to reduce it."[63] Similarly, an annual risk level of 1 in 1 million (or 10 million under special circumstances) is viewed as "the point at which an imposed risk can legitimately be treated as trivial by the decision-maker." The report notes a number of factors that should prevent rigid application of these numerical guidelines, such as the existence of especially sensitive subgroups or a clear causal link to a particular consumer product. Nonetheless, the study group's willingness to say that even risks as high as 1 in 1,000 might be acceptable under some circumstances seems surprising from the standpoint of the United States, where such numbers are more politically charged and hence used with greater caution. The Royal Society's readiness to propose a numerical measure of acceptable risk reflects the relatively unembarrassed way in which expert groups in Britain can tackle highly sensitive issues of social policy.[64]

However influential the Royal Society report may prove in the long run, its impact on current British policy is difficult to detect. The analytical procedures discussed in the report are not required by law or administrative guidelines in British toxic substances regulation. Though the term "risk assessment" is used by policymakers, it does not yet have fixed methodological connotations. In the context of occupational safety and health, for example, risk assessment means merely the informal evaluation of the nature and magnitude of hazard that employers are obliged to perform under the Health and Safety at Work Act of 1974. Risk assessment obligations under the Control of Lead at Work Regulations of 1980 amount to a requirement that employers monitor the degree and nature of worker exposure in order to determine whether there is a "significant" risk. These are essentially qualitative exercises designed to evaluate in broad terms the risks that arise in particular industrial processes. They bear little resemblance to U.S. efforts to estimate the risk of cancer from extremely low levels of exposure to individual substances.

The nebulous operational meaning of "risk assessment" in Britain is symptomatic of a decision-making system that generally places low reliance on formal methodologies. The vogue for carcinogenic risk assessment may also have been slow to develop in Britain because regulators are prepared to find practical thresholds of safety even for some carcinogens.[65] However, formal risk assessment models of the type applied to UFFI by CPSC have not been widely used anywhere in Europe, even in countries such as Germany where rigorous control of carcinogens is the norm. In explaining this divergence, some experts have suggested that quantitative risk assessment methodologies are most readily accepted in the United States because they were initially developed in this country.[66] The "not invented here" syndrome is a plausible explanation for cross-national differences on some technical issues.[67] But given the international diffusion of science, as well as the very real contributions made by European scientists to the development of carcinogenic risk assessment models,[68] this explanation does not seem satisfactory in the present case. It also begs the question of why quantitative risk assessment was invented in the United States in the first place. One must probe deeper to find convincing reasons for the remarkable reliance on risk assessment and other formal analytical techniques in U.S. regulation of carcinogens.

The comparison of chemical control policies by Brickman et al. uncovered suggestive links between the open and politically exposed position of U.S. regulatory officials and their preference for rigorous quantitative analysis.[69] In a system where controversial decisions must be made in public, adversarial forums, usually without benefit of supporting consensus-building mechanisms, officials may find the appearance of methodological rigor especially appealing. Techniques such as cost-benefit analysis and risk assessment make it easier to reassure critics within and outside government that policy decisions are being made in a rational, nonarbitrary manner.

The move to quantify risk has also drawn support in the United States from interests wishing to slow down or curtail federal regulation of carcinogens. In Europe and Canada, the tradition of decentralized, case-by-case decision-making ensures that government will not act overzealously or with equal energy on all fronts at once. The absence of similar bureaucratic controls in the United States creates a greater potential for overregulation. Regulated industries have therefore been sympathetic to analytical procedures that not only delay action on individual substances, but provide a possible basis for discriminating among greater and lesser hazards.

However, American interest groups and activist scientists are well aware that the uncertainties surrounding formal analytical methodologies can be exploited to justify very different political ends. This means that interest in any given analytical approach is apt to be short-lived. Thus, business and industry brought a number of lawsuits in the 1970s and early 1980s to force regulatory agencies to perform formal cost-benefit analysis.[70] The benzene case indicated a shift of attention to the area of risk assessment. But industry representatives now admit in private that the benzene case gave them at best a limited procedural victory.[71] As long as agencies go through the motions of carrying out risk assessments, industry expects that courts will uphold their policy judgments, even if the assessments are always based on conservative assumptions that tend to overstate the degree of risk. This outcome, however, would leave the chemical companies little better off than they were before the benzene case. This may explain why the petroleum industry apparently softened its demand for quantitative risk assessment in the benzene regulatory negotiation (see chapter 7). In the future, industry is increasingly likely to challenge risk assessments on methodological grounds, as the UFFI manufacturers did in their lawsuit against CPSC.

Even if mathematical modeling achieves greater currency in the decision-making of other Western countries, public discussion of alternative methodologies is likely to remain more perfunctory than in the United States. Technical debate will most probably be restricted to expert committees such as Britain's Royal Society. Unlike the U.S. rule-making process, most national regulatory systems do not routinely provide for public hearings on regulatory proposals. The public inquiry process in Britain and Canada, for example, is reserved for policy issues of exceptional social impact. Given the muted character of most scientific debate relevant to policy-making, risk assessment methodologies adopted by governmental agencies in other countries are likely to be accepted as "science" and to escape serious public criticism.

Another factor that would tend to limit debate on methodological issues is that it is significantly harder to challenge a governmental agency in court in countries other than the United States. The entry barriers against litigation are universally higher in both Europe and Canada, whether by virtue of rigid standing rules, vague definitions of the government's legal obligations, or a cost allocation system that puts losers at serious financial risk.[72] In parliamentary systems, moreover, executive agencies are viewed as accountable to the legislature rather than the judiciary. As a result, when public interest groups pursue legal challenges in court, they may find the judiciary reluctant to infringe upon the executive's power over policy-making. In a significant recent British case, for example, the House of Lords refused objectors the right to cross-examine government experts on the contents of the "Red Book"—a manual used to predict traffic density on motor-ways—on the ground that these were matters of governmental policy.[73] There is every reason to expect that an agency's choice of carcinogen risk assessment models would also be regarded as an unreviewable policy decision.

The decade-long controversy about regulating carcinogens offers unique opportunities for studying how different policy systems accommodate to changes in scientific knowledge. In risk management, as in many areas of governmental policy-making, public officials recognize the importance of predictability and continuity. A consistent policy approach is fair to affected parties—it tells them what to expect, and they can modify their behavior accordingly—and enhances the decision-maker's credibility. Advances in science, however, pose a fundamental challenge to continuity in the risk-management process, since new knowledge tends to undercut established assumptions about risk and to reveal errors in past policy decisions. The case of carcinogen regulation shows how policy-makers in different countries have sought to cope with this dilemma.

Scientific change is most easily accommodated in policy systems where risk decisions are made incrementally, on a case-by-case basis. For example, in Finland or West Germany, where risk management is based on a list of carcinogens, official policy can be updated fairly easily to incorporate information about new hazards. In revising these lists from year to year, the government's scientific advisers can use the latest studies and incorporate recent evaluations by IARC or other national and international agencies. The German classification scheme offers special opportunities for incremental decision-making, since substances can be moved from one hazard category to another as more information becomes available. Similarly, in Britain, Canada, and France, the absence of a comprehensive official policy for managing carcinogenic risk enables policy-makers to regulate new hazards as they are revealed and to preserve some flexibility in choosing among alternative doctrines of scientific assessment.

Another way to make policy decisions responsive to scientific change is to give scientists great autonomy in the selection and interpretation of scientific data. In most European countries, the task of identifying carcinogens is viewed primarily as a scientific exercise. Accordingly, advisory committees are not bound to follow any preordained policy guidelines in weighing the evidence on particular substances. The only serious constraint on a scientist's ability to use new information in such a setting is that the committee's collective judgment has to take precedence over any member's individual judgment.

The risk management approach favored in the United States presents greater problems from the standpoint of responding to scientific change. As discussed in chapter 2, U.S. decision-makers have preferred to make explicit the rules they expect to use in interpreting incomplete or conflicting data. The EPA cancer principles, the OSHA cancer policy, and the IRLG guidelines on carcinogen identification and risk estimation were all manifestations of a national preference for such "generic" policies. The rationale for adopting such principles is primarily administrative and political: to promote continuity and, by putting the public on notice, to introduce greater accountability in science-based decision-making. Inevitably, however, this approach leads to a certain loss of flexibility. Since these principles of scientific interpretation are adopted as formal statements of administrative policy, they are difficult to revise on short notice to reflect changes in scientific knowledge. The difficulty is not merely procedural, but also political. Private interest groups who have come to rely on a particular administrative approach to risk assessment may be reluctant to go along with attempted revisions, even if these revisions are motivated by advances in science.

Recent developments in U.S. carcinogen management policy suggest that in spite of these drawbacks the United States is not about to abandon its preference for formal principles of scientific interpretation. An instructive illustration is the major document issued by the Office of Science and Technology Policy (OSTP) in March 1985 under the title "Chemical Carcinogens: A Review of the Science and Its Associated Principles."[74] The OSTP document represents an effort to reduce the political conflict generated by earlier agency attempts to regulate carcinogens and to create a scientifically up-to-date basis for evaluating carcinogenic risk. OSTP is not itself a regulatory agency and, unlike OSHA's 1980 policy, the OSTP review explicitly dissociates itself from any intent to formulate regulatory policy or to standardize risk assessment methodologies. Nevertheless, the thrust of the OSTP document is similar to that of earlier U.S. cancer policies in that it attempts to derive from current scientific knowledge a set of *general* principles which can guide the regulatory agencies in considering carcinogens.[75] Moreover, simply by creating a unified framework for reviewing scientific data about carcinogens, the OSTP document will surely affect risk assessment practices in the agencies, thus indirectly influencing the development of regulatory policy.

As noted above, early U.S. policy on carcinogens tended to treat all such substances as equally hazardous. The Delaney clause illustrates this policy in extreme form, since it requires a blanket ban on certain classes of additives if they are shown to cause cancer in humans or animals. Recent advances in the field of analytical chemistry, cancer testing, and biostatistics have made it possible for regulators to discriminate more carefully among substances that meet the first blunt test of carcinogenicity, namely, that they increase the formation of neoplasms in some species. The flourishing field of risk assessment reflects a broad scientific and administrative consensus that it is no longer appropriate to treat all carcinogens alike.

Characteristically, the interest in risk assessment in the United States has led to a new round in the development of guidelines for decision-making. EPA, for example, thoroughly revised the risk assessment guidelines that had been in use at the agency since the late 1970s. The new document states how EPA will approach certain controversial issues in risk assessment as a matter of policy. For example, the agency expects to use the linearized multistage model for estimating risks at low doses for most carcinogens.[76] It appears that the focus on risk assessment, although driven by scientific change, has not altered the preference of U.S. regulators for a definite, principled approach to making science policy.

But how does the U.S. risk management system respond when scientific changes are so far-reaching that they cannot easily be incorporated into established bureaucratic approaches to decision-making? What is the impact of radical shifts in scientific thought on a policy system that is wedded to continuity and to firm guidelines for resolving controversies about risk? Some insights can be drawn from the reception in the United States of research that seems to undermine the foundations of U.S. cancer policy by suggesting that the emphasis on industrially produced chemical carcinogens has been misplaced.

The view that chemical carcinogens are worth special regulatory attention, at least if they present more than a *de minimis* risk, came under serious attack in a study commissioned by the U.S. Office of Technology Assessment from Richard Doll and Richard Peto, two of Britain's leading epidemiologists.[77] Specifically, their work denied the existence of a "cancer epidemic," at least after mortality rates are corrected for smoking and old age. Doll and Peto emphasized the importance of looking at the relative risk from different sources of exposure to carcinogens, noting in particular, that smoking and dietary factors together may account for up to 75 percent of all environmentally caused cancers in the United States. Beside this figure, the estimated risks of exposure to carcinogens in the occupational or general environment appear relatively insignificant. The study carried a clear message for regulators: to get the biggest bang for the cancer regulation buck, resources should be spent on controlling tobacco and diet rather than any other sources of exposure.

These findings have recieved pointed support from Bruce Ames, a prominent American biochemist, best known for his pathbreaking work on short-term tests for detecting chemical mutagens. Ironically, Ames's earlier research tended to reinforce the dominant regulatory focus on chemical carcinogens. The Ames test is one of the basic techniques used by governmental and industrial laboratories to establish the mutagenicity of toxic substances. It is also widely used in identifying carcinogens, since it is increasingly apparent that cancer begins with a mutation or genetic change in the cell. A positive Ames test result was an important factor in the Consumer Product Safety Commission's decision to ban Tris, a flame retardant.[78] At the time, Ames himself urged regulators to display more concern about substances showing positive results in short-term tests.[79] He also proposed that short-term tests be used for quantitatively estimating the mutagenic potential of different chemical substances.[80]

Ames's current research, however, has turned away from industrial chemicals and consumer products to the investigation of natural mutagens and carcinogens. Influenced by the correlations Doll and Peto discovered between diet and cancer, Ames concluded that one of the more fruitful avenues in modern cancer research is to study the interactions between dietary carcinogens and anticarcinogens.[81] The latter category consists of substances that protect cells from oxidation, believed to be a major source of damage to DNA. A thesis implicit in Ames's concern with these substances is that dietary mutagens and carcinogens, to which humans are exposed in larger numbers and larger concentrations than to industrial chemicals, deserve much greater attention than the synthetic chemicals which have preoccupied regulatory programs for most of the past fifteen years. Moreover, understanding the body's own defense mechanisms, particularly the role of anticarcinogens, could lead to better preventive policies than current strategies aimed at reducing exposure to individual chemical carcinogens.[82]

Although there is nothing inherently unreasonable about this research agenda, Ames's statements about diet and cancer have proved controversial. Environmentalists generally perceive his new line of research as inimical to the cause of public health protection. It appears to downgrade traditional areas of regulatory concern, such as hazards at work. The fear is that the relative risk arguments developed by Doll, Peto, and Ames will be exploited by advocates of deregulation and that resources will be diverted from controlling industrial carcinogens, even if significant numbers of workers are exposed to them each year. One well-known critic is Samuel Epstein, a scientist and political activist, whose own work strongly argues that American regulators have paid insufficient attention to the risks posed by chemical carcinogens.[83] In Epstein's view, interest in the dietary causes of cancer is misguided because it rests on an inflated appraisal of the cancer risk attributable to food.

The controversy between Ames and his environmentalist critics shows how easily new scientific paradigms can acquire broader social overtones in the United States. Ames himself has been quite explicit about the implications of his work on natural carcinogens, stating in numerous public forums that "nature is not benign."[84] The theme was picked up by *Science* magazine when it published Ames's early findings on carcinogens and anticarcinogens. The cover carried in bold graphics the message "EAT-DIE."[85] The suggestion was clear: Cancer is not produced by what you unwillingly breathe or touch or drink. It is a product of what you willingly consume as food. In a rather frightening way, you are what you eat.

In the context of U.S. cancer policy, the theme "nature is not benign" is not merely a neutral statement about nature. It carries the same overtones as industry's repeated contention that we do not live in a risk-free world and should not strive to eliminate all the risks of technological development. Moreover, the "eat-die" theme seems to implicate voluntary, individual lifestyles, rather than exposure to pollution, as the more significant cause of cancer. Industry has consistently played on both themes in its attempts to block or sidetrack regulation of synthetic compounds. Those who advocate stricter governmental intervention against technological risk hear these themes as calls to fatalistic acceptance of the status quo or as affirmations of the "blame the victim" explanation of disease. The scientific investigation of diet and cancer thus has found itself entangled from the start in a polarized debate about what risks are "natural" and how resilient the human oganism is against risk. In such an environment, it would be hard for scientists to maintain the appearance of objectivity even if they were more cautious with their rhetoric than Ames has been. Any relation one posits between cancer and the environment is bound to be perceived as morally colored and controversial, for, as Mary Douglas argues, "no one can impose a moral view of physical nature on another person who does not share the same moral assumptions."[86]

All of this points to an important difference between ordinary scientific activity and science carried out in a policy context. Kuhn characterizes "normal" science as puzzle-solving, with the choice of experimental and theoretical problems directed by the prevailing scientific paradigm. Fact-gathering, for example, is directed toward areas that the paradigm predicts are important or toward elucidating ambiguities in the paradigm.[87] In policy-relevant science, however, the questions scientists ask (or fail to ask) are not guided by a scientific paradigm alone, but by more instrumental considerations arising from the policy process. Thus, a number of areas in cancer research, such as the study of DNA adduct formation or DNA repair, have become interesting not only in their own right, but because they bear on questions raised by policy-makers about dosimetry or the existence of a threshold for exposure to carcinogens. The fields of mutagenicity testing, experimental toxicology, and biostatistics have all grown enormously in response to the demands of the regulatory system and the desire of chemical manufacturers to avoid products liability litigation.

When scientific knowledge emerges from a context in which research goals are openly tied to social concerns, its capacity to influence policy is substantially diluted. Both action and inaction fall under suspicion in policy-relevant science. The regulatory system's interest in closure and continuity can prevent the undertaking or utilization of research that tends to upset a bureaucratically acceptable approach to risk management. Throughout the U.S. cancer policy debate, for example, the chemical industry charged the agencies with "freezing" science into rigid guidelines that fail to keep abreast of new scientific knowledge.[88] But alleged advances in science can seem equally suspect, particularly when they are the work of scientists with an institutional commitment to weaker regulation of technology. From the standpoint of a labor or environmental group, for example, an industry scientist's search for species-specific mechanisms of cancer looks less like disinterested scientific puzzle-solving than like a conscious attempt to create uncertainty about the general principles used by agencies for extrapolating animal data to humans. The proliferation of such seemingly instrumental research in the policy arena has prompted some sociologists of science to argue that we should view scientific uncertainty as a political construct.[89] The skepticism that has greeted the research on diet and cancer illustrates a similar reaction.

The credibility of policy-related science is, of course, hardest to maintain in a cultural context where the social concerns underlying the choice of research problems and the selection of basic paradigms are most open to public view. This is the case in the United States, where law and tradition have combined to keep the communication lines among regulators, scientists, and the public unusually free. In countries where the scientific advisory system is more closed and self-contained, the interrelationships between science and policy are more difficult to discern, so that the lay public has fewer reasons to question the authoritativeness of expert opinions. The institutional and procedural framework of policy-making influences the behavior of the scientific community as well. American scientists, who are subject to open peer review and are often called upon to testify for particular political interests, appear quite prepared to challenge each other's assumptions openly in the course of policy disputes. Their European colleagues, by contrast, operate in a less adversarial and more credulous environment. Relatively untroubled by public challenges, European scientists find it easier than their U.S. counterparts to close the book on controversies relevant to policy and to prevent professional disagreements from turning into public arguments. These differences in the ability of scientists to contain expert conflict emerge with special clarity from the comparison of formaldehyde regulatory policies in the following chapter.

This chapter looks at the regulation of a single carcinogen, formaldehyde, to see how the differences in policy approach described in earlier chapters affect specific regulatory outcomes in several countries. The case is particularly interesting for comparative study because it is prototypical of the most difficult problems in chemical risk management. Formaldehyde, the twenty-sixth largest volume chemical in the United States, is a versatile substance, widely used in manufacturing a variety of products from plywood and home insulation to embalming fluids and cosmetics.[90] Exposure to formaldehyde can occur through several environmental pathways, as well as through food, tobacco smoke, and occupational contact. The chemical's carcinogenicity is known with reasonable certainty from rodent studies. The most persuasive study was carried out under the auspices of the Chemical Industry Institute of Toxicology (CIIT), a research center established by the chemical industry to test the effects of economically significant products.[91] Rats exposed to formaldehyde in the CIIT experiment contracted nasal cancer at two dose levels, with about half of the animals displaying disease symptoms at the

41

highest level of exposure (14.3 parts per million). Exposed mice showed a similar, but much smaller response, and only at the highest dose level. Based on these results, an IARC working group concluded in 1982 that "there is sufficient evidence that formaldehyde gas is carcinogenic to rats."[92] However, the concurrently available epidemiological evidence did not permit any reliable assessment of carcinogenicity in humans. Formaldehyde therefore squarely confronted regulators with questions about how to act when a substance presents only an indeterminate risk of cancer, but threatens a potentially large population.

In Germany, the DFG commission classified formaldehyde in Group B of its carcinogen list.[93] In other words, it is a substance "justifiably suspected of having carcinogenic potential," rather than a compound proved "unmistakably carcinogenic in animal experimentation." This conclusion was contrary to IARC's assessment that formaldehyde is definitely carcinogenic to rats. The scientific basis for the DFG commission's classification was therefore not completely transparent.

The regulatory consequences of a Group B classification are easier to evaluate. Currently, occupational exposure to formaldehyde in Germany is regulated by a MAK-value, or maximum exposure level, of 1 ppm. Classification in Group A2, the next higher risk category, would automatically have invalidated this exposure standard. As stated earlier, German cancer policy assumes that no "safe" threshold of exposure can validly be established for known animal carcinogens. If formaldehyde were shifted to Group A2, it would become the responsibility of the labor ministry, acting on the advice of its expert committee on hazardous substances, to develop a new exposure standard subject only to considerations of feasibility. This process could theoretically produce a stricter exposure limit than the existing 1 ppm, as well as additional monitoring and control requirements for industry. The decision to retain formaldehyde in Group B may have signified, at least in the DFG commission's opinion, that the evidence of carcinogenicity was too equivocal to justify a more stringent standard. Thus, although the classification of formaldehyde was a scientific decision rendered by a group of independent experts, it incorporated an unspoken policy judgment that the risks of formaldehyde were already under adequate control.

In Britain, occupational exposure to formaldehyde was regulated for some time by a threshold limit value (TLV) of 2 ppm based on the pre-1984 recommendations of the American Conference of Governmental Industrial Hygienists, an influential U.S. standard-setting organization. British labor unions complained that the TLV was exceeded in many workplaces and urged the government to adopt an official control limit for formaldehyde. Violation of a control limit usually entails more serious legal consequences for employers than failure to comply with the TLVs. The response of the Health and Safety Executive (HSE) was paradoxical. Under the Health and Safety at Work Act, control limits are generally adopted only on the basis of fairly unequivocal evidence that higher exposures will harm worker health.[94] Such evidence is simply not available for formaldehyde. In fact, new epidemiological data released by Britain's influential Medical Research Council (MRC) did not appear to support the view that formaldehyde is a human carcinogen posing a detectable threat to exposed workers.[95] Nonetheless, the Advisory Committee on Toxic Substances (ACTS) reconsidered formaldehyde in 1984 and recommended a control limit of 2 ppm. ACTS also proposed that exposure should be reduced further over time "so far as is reasonably practicable."[96] These recommendations were accepted by the Health and Safety Commission, the leading policy-making agency for occupational safety and health, and the new control limit came into effect at the beginning of 1986.

There are two points worth noting about this regulatory history. First, if indeed control limits are ordinarily reserved for substances posing a well understood threat to human health, then the formaldehyde case represented a departure from prior British regulatory practice. Yet industry representatives on ACTS obviously acquiesced in this change of policy, although it meant potentially more serious obligations for them in the future. The second point has to do with the consideration of science in making decisions about carcinogens. The precise connections between the scientific data and the control limit were never extensively discussed by ACTS. Indeed, given that the MRC epidemiological data did not confirm a risk to humans, ACTS had no obvious basis for treating formaldehyde as if it was a human carcinogen. The most plausible explanation for the new policy is economic rather than scientific. Regardless of the science, industry was prepared by 1984 to accept the 2 ppm control limit as "reasonably practicable." In any event, the British regulatory process succeeded in adopting a relatively tough posture toward formaldehyde without openly debating its carcinogenicity or getting deeply involved in any of the general scientific debates about carcinogenic risk. The outcome can be seen as a victory for political common sense, even though it may not have conformed to high standards of intellectual clarity.

Formaldehyde, in the form of UFFI, came to the attention of Canadian policy-makers during the energy crisis of the early 1970s.[97] The national government instituted a home insulation program that provided financial assistance to buyers of officially "accepted" insulation materials. In 1977, the agency responsible for implementing this program, the Canadian Mortgage and Housing Corporation (CMHC), decided to accept several UFFI products that conformed to a governmentally established manufacturing standard. There are indications that the standard-setting process was speeded up to meet the demands of the insulation program, even though questions were raised about UFFI's performance and safety. At any rate, the UFFI installation program was plagued almost from the start by consumer complaints about headaches, eye irritation, and respiratory difficulties, as well as doubts about UFFI's effectiveness as an insulant. In 1981, three years after CMHC's initial acceptance of UFFI, the product was banned by the Department of National Health and Welfare under authority of the Hazardous Products Act.[98] Unlike the ban proposed by the Consumer Product Safety Commission (CPSC) on UFFI in the United States, this action was not challenged in court. Two years later, Canada enacted special legislation establishing a federal compensation program for homeowners injured by the purchase of UFFI pursuant to the home insulation program.

The CIIT study clearly played a major role in the Canadian government's decision to ban UFFI. Shortly after the preliminary results from that study became available, Canadian authorities commissioned an evaluation of the health risks associated with formaldehyde from an ad hoc panel of U.S. and Canadian experts, including both toxicologists and allergists. Based on this committee's recommendations, a temporary ban was issued as early as December 1980 and the action became final a few months later. The five-member expert committee concluded in the first place that formaldehyde foam insulation is an unstable product. Upon deteriorating, the foam releases potentially dangerous quantities of formaldehyde gas into the air. This design defect, coupled with U.S. findings about the compound's allergic effects and possible carcinogenicity, led the committee to favor a ban on UFFI. Significantly, the committee did not consider the risk of cancer in isolation or make any effort to quantify it precisely. Carcinogenicity was merely one factor, along with the compound's remaining toxicological and physical properties, that influenced the committee's final recommendation to the Canadian government. Though the UFFI industry firmly opposed the ban, there is no evidence that it attempted to contest the committee's technical determinations.

Whereas agencies in Germany, Britain, and Canada dealt with formaldehyde only in a single regulatory framework, in the United States the substance attracted the attention of at least four major regulatory agencies: EPA, OSHA, CPSC, and the Department of Housing and Urban Development (HUD). In each case, the primary reason for concern was the suspicion, fueled by the CIIT study, that formaldehyde might be a human carcinogen. CPSC, the first agency to propose concrete action, issued a ban on the use of urea-formaldehyde foam insulation in 1982, but this was subsequently overturned by a federal Court of Appeals for lack of "substantial evidence."[99] Relying on essentially the same record, EPA and OSHA both decided as of mid-1983 that it was premature to take further regulatory action on formaldehyde.[100] These decisions gave rise to some of the most acrimonious debate about the relationship between science and policy since the controversy generated by the EPA and OSHA cancer policies of the 1970s. Under public pressure and in response to legal action, both agencies resumed regulatory consideration of formaldehyde in 1984.[101] During this period, HUD developed standards to control formaldehyde emissions from pressed-wood products used in constructing manufactured homes.

One result of these regulatory activities was to expose the scientific basis for assessing formaldehyde's carcinogenic potential to extensive review and comment. It became clear in the course of these proceedings that the advocates and opponents of regulation were exploiting the scientific uncertainties about formaldehyde to build arguments supporting radically different policy objectives. Those favoring more stringent control of formaldehyde generally emphasized its potential harm to human health. They noted that a relatively high risk to humans could be inferred from the compound's apparent genotoxicity and its unmistakable carcinogenicity in rats at doses comparable to actual levels of human exposure. Proregulation forces made much of epidemiological studies showing increases in cancer at sites other than the respiratory tract, but dismissed the negative studies for a variety of design defects. The absence of nasal cancer in exposed human populations was viewed as unimportant for several reasons. Experts noted, for example, that site concordance between animals and humans has not been found for all carcinogens, and that human respiratory behavior—including the tendency to breathe through the mouth when there are irritants in the air— differs substantially from the nose-breathing habits of rats.[102] Accordingly, one would expect airborne pollutants to affect the nasal passage much more readily in rats than in humans.

Turning most of these arguments on their head, representatives of the formaldehyde industry claimed that the negative epidemiological studies indicate, at the very least, that the upper limit of risk from formaldehyde is too low to justify serious regulatory concern. Some industry experts insisted, as well, that the absence of nasal cancer in exposed humans was quite significant. They argued that the negative human data, taken together with equivocal results in the mouse bioassays, suggest that there is a species-specific explanation for the nasal cancer observed in rats. One theory advanced by industry scientists was that cancer occurs in the rat only secondarily, as a result of damage inflicted by formaldehyde, a strong irritant, on cells in the rat's nasal lining. Comparable cell damage has not been observed in mice or in humans. A disproportionate increase in the rate at which rats develop cancer at very high exposure levels seems to give this theory additional support, since irritation also correlates with high exposures. Other scientists, however, found this explanation of the positive rat studies unpersuasive. They emphasized that although the irritant properties of formaldehyde may increase the risk of cancer at very high doses, this neither explains the formation of carcinomas in the first instance nor has a crucial bearing on the assessment of the risk to humans.[103]

These arguments and counterarguments underscore the exceptional difficulty of achieving closure on scientific issues in the U.S. regulatory process. There can be no doubt that open debate helps pinpoint the areas of uncertainty in the technical record, but this process leads eventually to disputes that simply cannot be resolved on the basis of existing scientific evidence. The highly active U.S. research system can be expected to keep producing new information about the carcinogenicity of formaldehyde. Yet increasing knowledge is often likely to create new frontiers of uncertainty, where the evaluation of evidence depends primarily on the interpreter's individual judgment and institutional or personal values. Thus, the potential for conflict may never be eliminated, only displaced to new technical arenas.

One example may help illustrate the point. While formaldehyde is unquestionably carcinogenic in rats, the results in mice are less conclusive. In the CIIT study, a small number of nasal carcinomas were observed in mice at the highest dose level, but these were not considered statistically significant. In discussing this fact at a congressional hearing, James Gibson, vice president of CIIT, made the following statement:

> An important perspective on the validity of the various models can be obtained by using the multistage model to predict tumor incidence in mice. Mice were exposed to formaldehyde simultaneously with rats in the CIIT study. If the rat data are used to predict nasal tumors in mice after 24 months of formaldehyde exposure to 15 ppm, 37 out of the 60 mice remaining at the 24th month should have had nasal tumors.
>
> Actually, only two mice developed nasal tumors and these were microscopic. Furthermore, their incidence was not statistically significant. Thus the rat data does not predict accurately the toxicity or carcinogenicity of formaldehyde in mice. This in turn calls into question the accuracy of the model for predicting carcinogenicity in man. Thus risk assessment across species, as from rat to mouse or to humans, is in most cases an extremely inexact procedure.[104]

EPA's discussion of the same facts in its proposed rule-making on formaldehyde took a rather different tack. In the agency's view,

> Although the two squamous carcinomas in mice at 14 ppm were not considered by the investigators to be statistically significant in comparison with the incidence in control mice in the study, the finding is considered by EPA to suggest that the effect is exposure-related because the natural background rate for such nasal cancers is very low in this strain of mice. The difference in susceptibility of rats and mice may be due, in part, to a greater reduction in respiratory minute volume (reduced volumetric

breathing rate) in mice than in rats during exposure to an irritating agent.[105]

There is no disagreement in these two statements about the nature of the observable effects, or even their statistical significance. But the CIIT representative and EPA do disagree on the all-important question of how to weigh the observed phenomena in the light of the total available evidence. The positions taken by the two sides differ sharply, though neither is obviously wrong or unscientific. In each case, the preferred interpretation is consistent with a predictable institutional bias: the CIIT scientist seeks to minimize the evidence of risk, while EPA analyzes the data from a more cautious, risk-averse point of view. The net result is a conflict which appears unanswerable, though it may provide an excuse for doing still more bioassays on other animal species.

In light of this continuing debate, the European response to the CIIT study appears singularly free from conflict. According to one European expert, formaldehyde was one of the first carcinogens to be regulated in Europe on the basis of a particular mechanism of cancer induction.[106] Specifically, in interpreting the CIIT results, European regulators accepted the theory that the damage inflicted by formaldehyde on nasal tissue accounts for the nonlinearity in the slope of the dose-response curve for rats at high exposure levels. In other words, they were persuaded that the degree of cell damage is the primary determinant of risk. Following this analysis, European experts concluded that the risk of cancer below the level at which injury to nasal tissue occurs may be real, since formaldehyde is mutagenic, but that this risk is not high enough for regulatory concern. To arrive at a "safe" exposure level for humans, European scientists therefore applied a traditional "safety factor" analysis to the rat data, extrapolating down a hundred-fold from the level at which tumor induction in the rat shows a sudden jump. In the United States, however, the safety factor approach is considered inappropriate in setting standards for carcinogens, since U.S. cancer policy does not admit the existence of safe thresholds for such substances.

The interesting point here is not merely that European agencies relied on a risk assessment model that has been widely criticized in the United States, but that their decision provoked hardly any scientific debate. In particular, there appears to have been no public challenge to the view that irritation of the nasal lining is the relevant "mechanism" of carcinogenesis for formaldehyde or that a safety factor approach can appropriately be used to control carcinogenic risk. There was no parallel in European scientific and regulatory circles for the thoroughgoing U.S. inquiry into alternative explanations of formaldehyde's carcinogenicity and competing risk assessment models. Even in Canada, scientific debate over the decision to ban UFFI was remarkably restrained, although governmental intervention carried serious economic consequences and was politically controversial.

The detailed elaboration of scientific arguments in American regulatory proceedings creates a superficial impression that policy decisions are grounded on a rational, factual basis. Legal provisions and judicial decisions feed the demand for rationality by requiring regulatory agencies to evaluate all the available technical data and to provide persuasive reasons for their actions. But the formaldehyde case suggests that these demands may simply create a scientific veneer for what remains in the end a subjective decision: When there is no conclusive scientific support for any particular policy choice, should the agency "tip the balance in favor of finding a human health risk or in favor of deferring such a finding until additional data are available?"[107] The decision is all the more subjective when it is unclear what benefits will be gained from postponing action. If the agency waits, will science come up with more definite answers? Or do the answers really lie beyond the capacity of current science in the sense described by Weinberg? How should policy-makers decide when scientists themselves cannot agree about whether an issue is "scientific," that is, capable of elucidation through science,[108] or inherently "transscientific"?

Following the EPA and OSHA's refusal to regulate formaldehyde in the early 1980s, some U.S. commentators have argued that decisions concerning the sufficiency of evidence should properly be characterized as "science policy."[109] Their legitimacy should then be judged by the criteria traditionally applied to policy decisions. For example, administrative responses to science policy questions should conform to legal standards of "reasoned decision-making." Did the agency pursue a course of action consistent with its legal mandate? Did it deviate from prior policy without adequate explanation? Did it follow proper procedures in making its policy determination?

Measured against these standards, EPA's 1982 decision not to consider formaldehyde pursuant to the Toxic Substances Control Act (TSCA)[110] falls substantially short of the mark. John Todhunter, then EPA's deputy assistant administrator for toxic substances, set forth his reasons for not acting in a memorandum which drew heavy criticism on both scientific and procedural grounds. Testifying before Congress, Dr. Norton Nelson, long-time director of the Institute of Environmental Medicine at New York University Medical Center, characterized the memo as "unusual and irresponsible" and "contrary to accepted scientific usage."[111] Other critics accused Todhunter of failing to comply with EPA's own established procedural requirements: consulting with a broad range of interests, explicitly explaining the departures from the agency's earlier cancer policy, and undertaking internal staff review or external scientific peer review.[112] According to Dr. Nelson and others, these deficiencies led to a hazard assessment document so one-sided that it could just as well have been prepared by the formaldehyde industry.

Like most significant regulatory controversies in the United States, the formaldehyde case engaged not only Congress and the scientific community, but also the courts, although with inconsistent results. The first judicial involvement with formaldehyde occurred when the manufacturers of UFFI successfully challenged CPSC's attempt to ban their product. In ruling that CPSC's proposed action was not based on "substantial evidence," the Court of Appeals for the Fifth Circuit found fault with the methods used by the agency to monitor exposure to formaldehyde and with the use of the rat cancer data alone to project risks for humans. Ironically, quantified risk assessments provided a basis for ordering agency action in a later lawsuit by the United Automobile Workers against OSHA. Proceeding under the Freedom of Information Act,[113] UAW forced OSHA to disclose the risk assessment it had commissioned for formaldehyde. OSHA's estimates of cancer risk proved high enough to persuade a court that the agency should be ordered to begin rule-making on formaldehyde.[114] At the same time, a lawsuit by the Natural Resources Defense Council prompted EPA to reconsider regulating formaldehyde under TSCA.[115] While these lawsuits did not generate new issues, they kept the scientific debate alive and encouraged opposing interest groups to go on regulating their basic adversarial arguments.

In late 1983, EPA created a novel scientific forum in an effort to close the spiraling scientific controversy about formaldehyde's carcinogenicity. The agency provided funds to the National Center for Toxicological Research (NCTR) to conduct a multidisciplinary workshop on formaldehyde. Eight scientific panels, each containing representatives from industry, government, and the universities, were asked to review different toxicological issues and to answer designated questions bearing on the regulation of formaldehyde. Though a consensus report was produced and circulated,[116] the workshop failed to end some of the debates that were most important to EPA. For example, the risk assessment panel could not reach a consensus on the most appropriate technique for estimating the risk of human exposure to formaldehyde on the basis of the data from the CIIT study.

Controversies provoked by EPA's advance notice of proposed rule-making on formaldehyde suggest that certain issues remain almost as unsettled as they were before the NCTR workshop. Arguments soon arose about the proper interpretation of the NCTR report. For example, the Formaldehyde Institute, the trade association representing the formaldehyde industry, accused EPA of paying insufficient attention to the role of cytotoxicity, or cell death, in inducing cancer in rats.[117] EPA justified its position on the ground that the relative contribution of this factor is unknown.[118] This exchange represents just one more round in the battle between those who want to find a particular mechanistic argument for dismissing positive animal data and those who believe that a risk to humans should be inferred from such data unless there is overwhelming evidence to the contrary.

From OSHA's standpoint as well, the consensus workshop failed to resolve some basic issues relevant to policy-making. The agency proposed new exposure standards for formaldehyde in December 1985.[119] The proposed rule provided for different standards depending on whether formaldehyde is determined to pose a carcinogenic risk to humans or not. This approach left the door open for continuing public debate about the carcinogenicity of formaldehyde.

Such long-drawn controversies over risk assessment decisions are hardly unprecedented in the United States. In the 1970s, for example, environmentalists sued the federal government over what they perceived as serious inadequacies in the environmental impact assessment of nuclear waste disposal.[120] Challenges to

EPA's evaluation of data on the carcinogenicity of the organo-chlorine pesticides led to the formulation of the agency's first in-formal "cancer principles."[121] More recently, the chemical indus-try has joined the attack on agency expertise, questioning the integrity and scientific judgment of federal administrators with respect to a host of regulatory activities, prominently including the generic cancer policies and assessments of particular carcino-gens.[122] These attacks, though mounted at different times by dif-ferent interest groups, represent at bottom a common complaint: that government's handling of technical information, particularly in areas of high uncertainty, is too often subverted by the political demands of special interests, in short, through "capture." The next two chapters explore the institutional and procedural means by which different national governments seek to avoid such an outcome.

In conclusion, the formaldehyde case illustrates some dra-matic cross-national differences in public responses to governmen-tal decisions about risk. In both Europe and Canada policy deci-sions were more readily accepted by industry and public interest groups than in the United States. Scientific debate, as well, re-mained at a minimum in public forums outside the United States. In contrast to American regulators, German, British, and Canadian authorities all reached quicker decisions with respect to formaldehyde, although they were operating with the same scientific data—and the same uncertainties—as their American colleagues. The reasons for their actions, however, were never completely articulated, so that the decisions leave something to be desired in terms of intellectual rigor. For example, although the issue of formaldehyde's carcinogenicity clearly played a part in both British and Canadian decision-making, regulatory authorities never explicitly assessed the risk of cancer or stated just how much importance they attached to this issue. Indeed, both Britain and Canada ultimately sidestepped the question of whether for-maldehyde should be treated as if it is a human carcinogen.

Yet the policy outcomes in Europe and Canada do not seem any less protective of health and safety than the initiatives under-taken in the United States. The German occupational exposure standard and the British control limit were both more stringent than the parallel OSHA standard for formaldehyde. The Cana-dian government successfully banned UFFI while CPSC was un-able to make its decision stick in court. Perhaps the largest irony is that after all the debate and all the experiments with scientific consensus-building, no U.S. agency came up with a definitive evaluation of the risk to human health presented by formaldehyde. In terms of effective government, then, the American regulatory system seems to have performed least satisfactorily. If there are benefits that offset the indecisiveness of the U.S. risk management process, they would seem to lie not so much in the realm of substantive policy as in the quality of the relations that risk management fosters among citizens, scientists, and the state.

One feature that clearly distinguishes modern risk management from past policy disputes is the increased demand by private citizens for a role in public decision-making.[123] Technological hazards not only threaten individual health and safety, but raise thorny distributive questions about apportioning the costs and benefits of development across societies and between present and future generations. Increasingly, citizens in the industrialized nations are reluctant to commit the resolution of such issues to the exclusive jurisdiction of experts and the state. The desire for greater participation is frequently coupled with demands for more decentralized decision-making, through local administrative proceedings or a local right to preempt policies developed by the central government. The search for procedures that will accommodate these concerns without destroying government's power to act has occupied legal scholars and policy analysts in both Europe and North America.

The pattern of participation that has developed in the U.S. risk management process differs notably from that in other Western countries. The differences are often described in terms of binary oppositions, which are heuristically useful, though admittedly oversimplified: the American participatory tradition is often characterized as formal, open, adversarial, and confrontational, while the European or Canadian approach is informal, confidential, consultative, and cooperative. These contrasts can be attributed in part to the extraordinary judicialization of the American administrative process in the past forty years. Agency rule-making in the United States has acquired many of the characteristics of a formal trial. As a result, individual citizens and citizen groups have unparalleled rights to intervene in administrative proceedings, to question the expert judgments of government agencies, and ultimately to force changes in policy through litigation.

These legal rights are bolstered by the openness of public access to information. Agencies must make regulatory decisions on the record, reviewing in detail the technical arguments for and against the selected course of action.[124] Much of the scientific advice obtained by agency officials from independent experts is available to the public pursuant to federal legislation regulating the conduct of advisory committees.[125] The Freedom of Information Act (FOIA) provides an additional legal avenue for compelling disclosure of information under the control of the agencies. The United Auto Workers' successful suit against OSHA in the formaldehyde case shows how FOIA can be used to combat agency inertia in the area of risk management.

Open public hearings or trial-type proceedings are occasionally used for developing risk management policies in countries other than the United States. As mentioned earlier, however, these procedures are usually reserved for issues of very broad public concern. The Berger Commission's public inquiry into the laying of a natural gas pipeline in Canada's Mackenzie Valley is one frequently cited example of participatory policy-making on a national scale. The inquiry's official purpose was to examine the economic, social, and environmental impacts of the pipeline, but its effect was much more broadly educational. Through a combination of several different kinds of hearings, Mr. Justice Berger succeeded not only in informing policy-makers and the public, but in helping affected communities to form and articulate their own opinions on the pipeline controversy.

In Britain, a massive public inquiry was held in 1977 to evaluate the government's plan to construct a $1.2 billion reprocessing plant for spent nuclear fuels at a site called Windscale. The hundred day Windscale inquiry was much less effective than the Berger inquiry in illuminating the political aspects of the proposed policy and in securing effective public participation.[126] Nevertheless, the Windscale experience provides another notable example of judicial procedures being used to explore the uncertainties and technical complexities surrounding a major risk management decision.

Apart from such sporadic cases, however, administrative systems in other Western countries have generally resisted the wave of judicialization that has swept across the American regulatory process. British administrative law experts, for example, have discussed the pros and cons of citizen suits, class actions, and freedom of information legislation for many years, but the debates thus far remain largely academic.[127] The German environmental movement spurred wide-ranging discussions about the legality and practicality of granting public interest associations the right to sue governmental agencies. In the end, however, German legal opinion concluded that such a relaxation of present standing rules could not be permitted in a tradition that regards lawsuits against the state solely as a means of protecting private rights against unlawful governmental intervention.[128] Canadian administrative procedures, as well, have retained their fundamentally consultative orientation, though Canada is perhaps more sensitive to U.S. developments than are other parts of the English-speaking world. Unlike Britain, Canada has enacted a freedom of information law, but with more limitations than its U.S. counterpart.

In several recent comparative studies of regulation, American scholars have argued that the cooperative, consultative approach to decision-making in other countries leads to more decisive and cost-effective policy outcomes than are achieved in the United States. One point of departure for this analysis is the cross-national record on regulating toxic substances. In their four-country survey of chemical control policies, Brickman et al. found that significant regulatory endpoints, such as the number of carcinogens subjected to public control, seem roughly comparable in all four countries over time.[129] Badaracco's case study of vinyl chloride regulation reaches a similar conclusion,[130] although Jasanoff's analysis of the vinyl chloride case points out that there were important variations in the timing and flexibility of the controls adopted in different countries.[131] Working on a much larger canvas, Vogel has tried to demonstrate that the British approach to environmental regulation has proved as effective as the American, though with lower expenditures and political turmoil.[132] The formaldehyde case discussed in the preceding chapter also suggests that the American risk management process is exceptionally slow in reaching decisions and invests disproportionate time in attempting to resolve essentially unresolvable scientific issues.

Examples like these have prompted some analysts to speculate that the admittedly much higher costs of regulatory proceedings in the United States may not yield sufficient returns in terms of public health or environmental protection and that U.S. regulators might do well to imitate certain institutional and procedural features that foster cooperation in other countries. Indeed, several regulatory agencies, including EPA and OSHA, have been driven by this logic to experiment with consensus formation on specific regulatory issues, though, as we see below, such efforts have met with only limited success.

From the vantage point of U.S. scholars, other Western nations seem to have developed a remarkably wide range of effective consensus-building mechanisms. The multipartite expert group, frequently encountered in European and Canadian risk management systems, is a particularly striking example. Unlike U.S. scientific advisory committees, which are ordinarily composed of technical experts unaffiliated with particular political interests, expert groups in Europe and Canada often include a contingent of interest group representatives who are not themselves research scientists. Typical examples are Britain's tripartite Advisory Committee on Toxic Substances and the German labor ministry's advisory committee on chemicals in the workplace.[133] The function of nonscientists on such bodies is to counteract the possibly unconscious biases of the trained scientists and to ensure that committee decisions reflect a range of values as well as technical knowledge. The possibility of negotiating value differences together with scientific differences is particularly appealing in areas of uncertainty such as carcinogenic risk assessment, where questions of fact and judgment are inextricably merged. By openly injecting values into technical debate, pluralistic expert negotiations can also guard against the temptation to justify basic value choices in terms of post-hoc scientific arguments. The tendency toward such artificial use of science is more difficult to avoid in the U.S. regulatory process, where policy-makers are under enormous pressure to demonstrate the rationality of their policy decisions.

Lay participants in various consensus-oriented processes, however, question whether these theoretical benefits are fully realized in the actual workings of multipartite advisory bodies. In their experience, credibility and hence power are often tied to technical mastery, so that "experts" whose sole contribution is in the "soft" area of values ultimately exercise little influence on the group's deliberations. Procedural decisions taken by the group as a whole can further dilute the impact of the nonscientific minority. For example, the Canadian expert committee reviewing the pesticide Captan took the position that minority reports should be written only as an action of last resort.[134] British tripartite committees, such as ACTS, likewise make no provision for formal minority opinions.[135] Indeed, the tradition of consensual decision-making in Britain dictates that a united front should be presented behind documents that are formally "agreed." A minority member who violates this tacit understanding, and talks to the media or otherwise makes disagreements public, is likely to be perceived as a maverick and to lose credibility. The norm of group solidarity is so deeply ingrained that labor representatives on ACTS cannot even count on support from higher union authorities if they choose to publicize their grievances against the rest of the committee.

These factors help explain why many Europeans believe that American studies of business-government relations substantially overestimate the extent of consensus in their countries. While natural social adversaries like business and labor may reach accommodations, this is not necessarily equivalent to a consensus. The mere fact that a decision is reached need not signify a real accord; often, the weaker adversary simply capitulates when an unpalatable outcome is backed by a more powerful opponent acting in alliance with government. In such cases, the fact that decisions are channeled through "consultative" or "cooperative" institutions is particularly misleading because it perpetuates the semblance of consensus without the substance. Given the realities of regulatory negotiation, non-American analysts argue that "consensus" is an empty concept and should be abandoned in favor of "cooptation" or "compromise."[136]

In analyzing the legal consequences of Canada's decision first to approve and then to ban UFFI, David Cohen presents a thoughtful critique of the consultative approach to standard-setting.[137] His observations are based on the activities of the Canadian General Standards Board (CGSB), whose committees and working groups played a key role in certifying UFFI for acceptance as a home insulation material. Not untypically, CGSB's UFFI committee was only selectively multipartite. It contained representatives from governmental departments, public utilities, and producing companies, but none from consumer groups or competing industries. With seven of its twenty-two members coming from industry, the possibility that a "significant majority" of the committee would oppose the producer interests was greatly diminished. CGSB's technical committee drew its data on UFFI almost entirely from producing companies, thereby strengthening industry's influence on the final decision. Under these conditions, as Cohen notes, a convergence of interests between governmental bureaucrats and industry was sufficient to ensure that UFFI would be certified as an acceptable product. In this case, government's interest in rapidly launching its home insulation program coincided so well with the business interests of the UFFI companies that doubts about the product's safety and efficacy were set aside. Cohen describes the resulting dynamics on the committee as follows:

> [T]hrough reliance on industry research data and expertise, and with a substantial portion of industry members, the committee decision-making processes conform to a rather unique modification of the "capture" theory of regulation. The capture in this case is a subtle process involving a weighting of industry representatives on the committee, the existence of parallel values and objectives, and a radical imbalance in information.[138]

Given the close business-government relations that develop in consultative systems, it is not surprising that risk management policies are often resistant to the initiatives of labor and public interest groups. According to one downbeat account of British chemical regulation, labor failed to win numerous major policy battles between 1980 and 1985 in spite of paticipating in a tripartite institutional framework. By 1985, no officially agreed list of occupational carcinogens had yet been established, although a preliminary list was included in the draft policy for the Control of Substances Hazardous to Health (COSHH). Several years of intense political activity brought no new framework for worker involvement in pesticide regulation. A new guidance note on chemicals in the workplace[139] provided for exposure limits that were higher in some cases than the most recent TLVs recommended by ACGIH (the American Conference of Governmental Industrial Hygienists). Attempts to create an Industrial Advisory Committee to study occupational hazards in the pharmaceutical industry were blocked by manufacturers. As of 1984, employers still had no legal obligation to monitor toxic substances in the workplace, so that there was no reliable mechanism for obtaining useful data on exposures.

It would be misleading, of course, to suggest that labor scored no gains in the period from 1980 to 1985. The Health and Safety Commission's decision to develop the COSHH policy must be seen as an important step forward, especially since it provides the authority for future regulation of carcinogens. Although the new guidance note contains some standards that are less stringent than those proposed by ACGIH, the mere development of a British list of TLVs creates new opportunities for labor to participate in standard-setting. These advances, however, have been slow to take shape and must seem, from labor's viewpoint, disappointingly incremental.

Multipartite negotiation plays a much more limited role in U.S. regulatory policy. It is recognized as a useful process but usually as a prelude to rather than a substitute for formal rule-making. Nicholas Ashford, for example, writes favorably of the achievements of a "balanced" advisory committee established under the Occupational Safety and Health Act:

> OSHA's twelve-member permanent committee, NACOSH [the National Advisory Committee on Occupational Safety and Health], has been a major forum for discussing and clarifying controversial issues before unnecessary adversarial interactions occur. For example, NACOSH investigated the idea of adopting a generic cancer policy long before OSHA had promulgated any formal rule. The committee served as an intellectual testing ground, and a review of its public transcripts reveals penetrating discussions of difficult questions on the science-law interface.[140]

As Ashford observes, the effectiveness of committees like NACOSH depends on their steady accumulation of expertise, experience, and public trust. If agency officials do not want such committees to develop into alternative centers of power, they can easily undermine the group's effectiveness through such tactics as rapid rotations in membership or drastic reductions in the number and frequency of meetings. OSHA's use of some of these strategies against NACOSH in recent years underscores the precarious role of multipartite bodies within the U.S. agency structure. In any event, since multipartite committees supplement, but do not supplant, the adversarial rule-making process, any consensus reached in such a forum is inherently unstable. The fact that NACOSH approved the concept of a generic cancer policy, for example, did little to alleviate the scientific and political conflicts that surfaced during subsequent rule-making proceedings.

The concept of "regulatory negotiation" has been discussed in U.S. policy circles as an alternative to formal rule-making. In the area of risk management, U.S. agencies usually follow a hybrid rule-making procedure that incorporates numerous features of a judicial trial. The process is best suited to developing and testing factual evidence. Experts appear as witnesses for opposing parties, and formal testimony is presented and often subjected to cross-examination. Critics of this approach note that the emphasis on fact-finding is inappropriate for most risk controversies, where the debated issues lie more in the domain of policy than fact.[141] Negotiation seems a more promising procedure for resolving the value conflicts inherent in disputes about technological risk.

Philip Harter, an early proponent of regulatory negotiation, argues that this procedure is also more democratic than the current administrative process: negotiation demands direct participation by those concerned with the policy outcome, whereas formal rule-making gives a governmental agency the authority to strike the final, possibly arbitrary balance among competing political interests.[142] The negotiation process draws opposing parties into a working relationship, often leading to a narrowing of the issues in dispute and a softening of positions on areas that still remain controversial. Negotiation has already provided practical benefits in some areas of environmental dispute resolution, such as siting controversies.

With these considerations in mind, OSHA sponsored a negotiated standard-setting process on benzene after the Supreme Court invalidated the exposure standard promulgated by the agency in 1978. Two consultants were appointed to mediate between the petroleum industry and concerned labor unions.[143] Discussions took place between October 1983 and August 1984, but it was understood by both parties that OSHA should continue work on its own regulatory proposal on benzene during this period. Despite the optimism generated at several stages in the negotiation process, it ended without any accord among the parties. OSHA also failed to meet its scheduled deadlines for issuing a preliminary standard by February 1984 and a final standard by June of the same year, although the delay was probably due to political rather than technical considerations. The agency published a proposed standard of 1 ppm in late 1985 following high-level administrative changes at the Department of Labor.[144]

From the accounts of several participants in the benzene negotiations it is clear that the health risks presented by the substance played a very minor role in the discussions. The petroleum industry demanded no new risk assessments, although it had argued before the Supreme Court that the OSHA standard should be invalidated because of the agency's failure to perform an adequate quantitative assessment of risk. There was also general agreement that the exposure standard should be set at 1 ppm, a level previously contested by industry in its lawsuit against OSHA. The benzene negotiation thus bears out the hypothesis that the undue elaboration of scientific arguments in the U.S. regulatory process is in part a product of the adversarial, litigation-oriented style of rule-making. Clearly, both parties recognized the inherent limitations of formal risk assessment, and, once relieved of the need to make a watertight legal argument about risk, neither side felt compelled to raise serious questions about the toxicity of benzene. The question was not whether it should be more strictly regulated, but how.

With the scientific issues largely set aside, differences among the parties shifted from the numerical exposure level to other aspects of the standard, such as the extent of the industry's obligation to medically monitor exposed workers, and above all on the policy to be followed by OSHA in enforcing the standard. In exchange for accepting the 1 ppm exposure limit, industry proposed a new way of determining whether a particular workplace was in violation. If routine sampling by OSHA disclosed that the standard had been exceeded, then the company would be permitted to establish on the basis of its own sampling records that the average level over the past *five* samplings was within the lawful limit. This averaging technique, industry argued, would protect firms against being prosecuted on the basis of a single aberrant sampling. The unions, however, found this approach unacceptable, viewing it as a further impediment to OSHA's already difficult task of citing companies for violating toxic substance standards.

Different parties offer different reasons for the eventual breakdown of the benzene negotiations. Industry's line of explanation generally blames labor's persistent lack of trust for the failure to reach an acceptable compromise. According to this view, the unions were reluctant to accept a relaxed enforcement policy for benzene because they feared this would set a precedent for future carcinogen standards. More important, industry representatives believe that labor was unwilling to live with an enforcement scheme in which decisions to prosecute would ultimately depend on data supplied by industry. Labor representatives analyze the situation differently. They blame the final impasse partly on structural problems in the negotiating process. While the unions represented themselves directly on one side, four trade associations stood in for the employer interests on the other. This meant that the industrial negotiators were not authorized to make binding proposals, but had to take them back to the member companies for approval, with a resulting loss of continuity in their deliberations with the labor groups. As far as the averaging proposal was concerned, labor claims that there was no good reason to countenance such a departure from established OSHA policy. Labor's final decision to stand tough was no doubt also helped by new epidemiological findings about the effects of low-level exposure to benzene. With scientific support growing for the existence of a risk even at low levels, labor interests felt that they were in a stronger position on the health issue and could press for a more advantageous standard through traditional rule-making.

Most of the problems mentioned by the parties do not appear fatal to the concept of regulatory negotiation. The most appropriate parties to a negotiation are undoubtedly harder to identify in the United States than in Europe, where major interest groups are more tightly and hierarchically organized in the neocorporatist mode. But the structural problem does not seem impossible to overcome even in the United States, especially in the area of worker protection, where the parties are relatively few in number, and suitable "peak" organizations are therefore easier to find. Moreover, the scientific evidence of a health risk is more uncertain for most toxic substances than for benzene. Ambiguities in the science would tend to make the parties more responsive to a negotiated settlement.[145]

Much more problematic for the future of regulatory negotiation is the fact that labor objected not merely to the substance of industry's proposals about benzene, but to the process itself. One labor participant notes that long experience with collective bargaining has made mediation familiar territory to unions.[146] Nevertheless, she considers the process entirely unsuitable for standard-setting. In contrast to formal rule-making, negotiation is completely fluid. It builds no record and offers no clear means of holding the opposing party to particular factual findings or policy concessions from one meeting to the next. Some labor leaders are convinced, as well, that rule-making on the record makes for a tighter, more comprehensive standard than is developed through negotiation in other countries. This outcome is worth the expense and delay of formal hearings. Finally, rule-making, as an open, public process, offers a vehicle for educating organized labor's larger constituency. Regional meetings are held in connection with major rule-making proceedings, often eliciting new supporting data. These advantages would be lost in a more closed, consensual process.

Labor's objections to negotiated standard-setting underscore the close connections between a country's administrative process and its political culture. In their seminal cross-national study of political cultures in the early 1960s, Almond and Verba found that the "subjective political competence" of U.S. citizens—that is, their confidence in being able to influence governmental activities—was higher than that of citizens in Germany, Italy, Mexico, or even Britain.[147] It seems entirely consistent that the preference for open and adversarial administrative procedures should also be most strongly developed in the United States. Through such procedures, citizens not only have formal opportunities to influence policy-makers, but also have access to the information they require in order to exercise real influence. Information is particularly important in technically esoteric areas of decision-making, since the ability to prevent a particular policy outcome often hinges on the ability to come up with a credible scientific counterargument.

In more traditional consultative systems, the power to regulate the policy agenda and the flow of information remains in the hands of governmental agencies. Governmental control over these

65

key aspects of decision-making forces a degree of passivity upon even those citizens who are directly drawn into the consultative process. Appeal to a wider constituency is usually impossible without "going public," a course of action that is outside the rules of the consultative game and can result in the ultimate penalty: exclusion from future deliberations. In contrast, the judicialized U.S. process offers an accepted way of taking a "case" before the public so as to mobilize the latent political competence of those affected by the policy outcome. Without such procedures at their disposal, activists wishing to challenge administrative authority in Britain, for example, have no way of arousing their potential constituencies out of the "persisting deferential and subject orientations" noted in that country by Almond and Verba.[148]

A successful "civic culture," in the sense described by these authors, requires a balancing of disparities. Too great involvement by citizens can produce excessive demands on government, undercutting its capacity to act. Too little involvement permits government to proceed unchecked by any form of democratic control. The ideal civic culture is conceived as a dynamic phenomenon, permitting cyclical patterns of "disinterest-involvement-influence-withdrawal."[149] Judging from the record of risk management in the United States, it is arguable that the judicialization of the administrative process has tilted the balance too far in the direction of active citizen participation, producing paralysis in the decision-making process. In other countries, however, the consultative mode of resolving risk disputes leads very possibly to alienation or despair on the part of activists and to passive acceptance of governmental and scientific elites by most members of the public.[150]

Comparing consensus-building mechanisms across several countries shows that people holding widely divergent scientific or political views can be brought together only with great difficulty, if at all. Skepticism about the meaning of "consensus" under these circumstances is thoroughly justified. Yet in spite of their imperfections and limitations, mechanisms that encourage negotiation offer the greatest promise of allowing participation without bringing government to a halt. Multipartite negotiations can lead to stable and effective policy proposals when certain preconditions are met: the issues involve values and preferences rather than facts,[151] the group starts with a reasonable amount of common ground, and its members are persuaded that a collective decision will further a larger community of interests than the proposals advanced by any single party. Regulators can do much to create these preconditions if they are genuinely committed to obtaining results. They can define an overall strategy, cut off alternative policy choices, and raise the costs of reaching no decision or of subverting the negotiating process through litigation or direct political action. In some countries, the possibility that the regulatory agency will go ahead and issue an independent decision may prod disaffected parties into negotiating in good faith. In the United States, however, the administrator's freedom to take such unilateral action is circumscribed by legal requirements that all viewpoints be considered and explanations be provided for selecting a particular course of action.

The formaldehyde case illustrates how governmental attempts to regulate the risks of carcinogenic substances are beset to varying degrees by expert controversies about the interpretation of scientific data. Yet the vision of science as a source of policy guidance retains extraordinary appeal, and science continues to play a central role in the public justification of risk management decisions. Indeed, a large part of the official effort to resolve risk controversies is directed toward the design of institutions and procedures that improve the scientific basis for regulatory actions. In particular, governmental agencies are always under pressure to ensure that the science they have relied on is sound and uncolored by political bias. This chapter looks at the way two relatively neutral sources of expertise—the independent scientific community and international organizations—are involved in validating science-based decisions in different countries.

The relative authority of independent scientists in the risk management process depends to a large extent on prevailing national conceptions about the sociological foundations of scientific knowledge. Research in the sociology of science has led to at least two formulations of the degree to which science is socially constructed.[152] The dominant and more complex view holds that scientific knowledge is constructed partly in accordance with norms internal to science, such as empirical testing and peer review, but partly also in accordance with external social interests, including the political interests of particular scientific communities. The relative importance of the internal and external norms can vary across disciplines, over time, and in response to the political context. A more extreme formulation of the "social construction" hypothesis holds that differences in scientific claims can be reduced to differences in political orientation, so that most assertions about science can be seen as just a camouflage for constellations of values and preferences.

Understandably, the second formulation has found adherents among political activists, who sometimes claim that there is no such thing as "good" or "bad" science, at least in the policy context. All policy-relevant science, in this view, is directed to strategic ends, and its quality is irrelevant so long as it leads to the desired social objectives. At the opposite pole, some scientists are convinced that "good" and "bad" or "right" and "wrong" are absolute, unambiguous categories in science and that policymakers must steer clear of "scientific nonsense" if they are to reach legitimate policy decisions. In the words of one cancer epidemiologist, "If the Pope had been right and Galileo wrong we could hardly view their debate in the same light."[153]

These contrasting positions entail quite different consequences for the institutional framework of risk management, and particularly for the role of independent scientists in the policy process. If the assessment of risk is seen largely as a social and political construct, then the choice among conflicting scientific analyses can safely—and democratically—be delegated to political officials or pluralistic decision-making bodies. On the other hand, if risk assessment consists mainly of issues that science can resolve according to its internal standards, then the decision-making process should delegate such issues to scientists and allow them to be decided free from political influence.

On the whole, U.S. risk management practices have displayed considerable sensitivity to the social foundations of science, particularly to the charge that there are value controversies latent in many seemingly technical disputes about risk. Throughout the

1970s, U.S. public interest groups argued for broader lay participation in regulatory decisions to offset the personal or institutional preferences which they believed industry and agency scientists were injecting into the interpretation of technical information. A series of judicial decisions mandating greater openness and public participation in agency decision-making led to a high-water point for popular control of policy-relevant science and for the incorporation of democratic values into technical analyses of risk.

The flaw in this approach emerged only gradually, but could no longer be ignored by the early 1980s.[154] While public participation provided some safeguards against extreme political bias or other forms of prejudice in scientific decision-making, it proved ineffectual against administrative manipulation of scientific data to suit predetermined policy objectives. The history of chemical regulation contains numerous abuses of this latter kind, from virtual manufacturing of data[155] to the use of "scientific" classifications for carcinogens with no basis in the theory of cancer causation (see chapter 3). These incidents made it clear that both the proponents and the opponents of regulation were capable of distorting science in order to achieve their policy objectives.

One response to these troublesome discoveries, particularly in the United States, has been to try to draw a sharper dividing line between the responsibilities of scientists and policy-makers in risk evaluations. This is essentially the approach that the National Academy of Sciences (NAS) endorsed in the report on risk management discussed in chapter 4. The NAS panelists concluded that the integrity of science can best be protected by clearly separating risk assessment from risk management. The principles of risk assessment should be articulated by scientists with no thought to the management consequences, and assessments for individual toxic substances should be completed before any policy considerations come into play.

The problem with implementing these recommendations is that risk assessment, as currently conceived, contains too many uncertainties to be undertaken as a purely "scientific" exercise. In a working paper written for the NAS panel,[156] Lawrence McCray pointed out that few experts are prepared to characterize any part of risk assessment as primarily science. A typical cancer risk assessment consists of up to fifty separate steps, and as one proceeds through the phases of hazard identification, dose-response assessment, and exposure assessment, the "policy" component of the assessment process increases steadily. Scientific judgment must be exercised throughout, usually in full knowledge that different choices may lead to substantially different policy recommendations. Given this state of affairs, it is almost inevitable that a scientist's personal and political values will influence his reading of particular facts. The different interpretations placed by EPA and CIIT on the mouse data for formaldehyde are but one example of the divergences that may arise among scientists with different institutional interests. The attempt to maintain a clean conceptual divide between risk assessment and management thus looks unpromising at best.

An approach that some policy analysts favor more highly is to think of risk regulation as consisting of three distinct phases rather than merely two: technical assessment, "science policy," and finally pure policy.[157] The advantage of this conceptual scheme over that advocated by NAS is that it openly recognizes the existence of a gray area between the "mostly scientific" and the "mostly political" ends of the decision-making process. Proponents of this approach believe that "science policy" should be regarded as a special subcategory of policy decisions and should be subject to the general institutional and legal controls that ensure legitimacy in U.S. policy-making. In particular, while purely technical debates may safely be left to experts, science policy decisions should be exposed to democratic and judicial as well as scientific checks. Thus, critics of EPA's 1982 decision not to regulate formaldehyde under TSCA §4(f) argued that the agency's principles for carcinogenic risk assessment were "science policy" and should not have been altered without scientific peer review and public justification.

Recognizing that some decisions about science must be made in the open, under procedural controls, does not fully resolve the problems of institutional design nor clarify the relative roles of scientists and policy-makers. To begin with, as McCray's analysis suggests, there are no well-defined boundaries between "science," "science policy," and "policy" in the risk assessment process. This means that administrative agencies will not be able to find a principled basis for answering some key questions about the evaluation of risk information. For example, when is it appropriate to treat an issue as mainly scientific and to entrust it entirely to technical advisers? What are the features that mark issues as "science policy" and necessitate additional public participation? And when is it permissible to circumvent the scientific advisory system altogether, as Todhunter sought to do in his review of formaldehyde, because the decision seems to involve only policy?[158] Since different answers to these questions may produce substantially different regulatory results, one can expect them to generate rancorous debate. Yet the only acceptable answers may be those which emerge following such debate, as a result of negotiations among scientists, administrators, and concerned political interests.

Science policy issues by definition involve mixed determinations of science and policy. It is not immediately obvious, however, what kinds of institutions and procedures the agencies should use to ensure that such policy determinations are both scientifically and politically legitimate. The concept of "peer review" (or "independent scientific review") has recently gained ground in the United States as the preferred means of validating the scientific component of science policy decisions. There is a general recognition that technical data and assessments prepared by agency staffs should be submitted to some sort of scientific review. While Congress has mandated a form of peer review for some regulatory programs,[159] many still operate without such statutory requirements. The recurrent controversies of the past ten years have led most agencies to conclude that peer review would be a useful procedure to include in the rule-making process. It is understood as well that peer review of policy-relevant science must look very different from peer review of journal articles and grant applications. For example, the former process cannot follow the confidential or "double blind" formats adopted in the grants or journals context. Beyond this, however, ground rules have yet to be developed for creating a review process that is well adapted to the special characteristics of science in the regulatory domain.[160]

In Europe and Canada interest in establishing the boundaries between science and policy has been markedly lower than in the United States. One factor that helps defuse the demand for separating technical and value issues in other countries is the tradition of multipartite expert decision-making. Lay interests represented on pluralistic bodies and enjoying the power to influence regulation are not likely to balk at the prospect of mixing technical and policy considerations, particularly when other forms of

73

public participation are ruled out. Technical experts, too, have little to complain of, since their values tend to predominate over those of participants with no technical training (see chapter 7). But expert groups are often only partly representative, as in the case of CGSB's working committees or the DFG commission on toxic substances in the workplace, where labor, consumers, and environmentalists are not included. Although ACTS is a tripartite body, many of Britain's scientific advisory committees contain no political representation at all. Examples include the influential Advisory Committee on Pesticides, the Committee on the Safety of Medicines, and numerous scientific subcommittees whose role is to advise the expert groups with formal decision-making authority. As the formaldehyde case suggests, such nonrepresentative scientific advisory bodies in other countries make determinations that are, by American standards, impermissibly tainted with policy considerations. The fact that science policy decisions made by such groups are accepted by politicians and the public reflects a continuing tolerance for government by technical elites.

Public acceptance of risk management by experts may be inescapable in systems where scientific knowledge is the privilege of the few and trust in expertise is correspondingly high. But scientists participating in European decision-making believe that they have earned this trust. Their judgment is that elite advisory bodies can operate with a stricter adherence to scientific standards and a clearer sense of the public interest than can the more politically vulnerable agency staffs in the United States. When experts are given a free hand in assessing risk, public discord over science is kept to a minimum, and cases of fraud or misuse of technical information are infrequent. It is difficult to verify these claims without studying the records of advisory committees in detail—a task made difficult by the absence of written documentation. But the broad-brush comparisons undertaken in this monograph suggest that there are indeed some positive trade-offs associated with wide reliance on scientific expert committees. Consensus and scientific credibility to some extent offset incrementalism and a relinquishing of public involvement in technical decisions with a pronounced value component.

Whatever the costs of relegating risk management to technical experts, labor and public interest groups outside the United States are unlikely to press for reforms that would shift more power into the hands of the civil servants that staff the regulatory agencies. Though attitudes to the bureaucracy differ from one country to another,[161] there is no indication that the public in most European countries views its administrative elite with any greater or lesser trust than its scientific one. In any event, administrators in most countries would be extremely reluctant to make the kinds of public assumptions that some U.S. agencies have made in the name of "cancer policy" or "science policy." In systems where risk management controversies have successfully been delegated to scientific advisory committees, administrators are unlikely to jeopardize their own political credibility by actively seeking more control over such decisions.

International organizations have established a strong presence in the field of chemical regulation, and with growing global interdependence their role is not likely to diminish. The activities of specific institutions and expert groups have been amply documented in the policy literature. It is clear from these accounts that international organizations have an indispensable part to play in facilitating the production and transfer of information about chemical hazards. The Organisation for Economic Cooperation and Development (OECD), for example, sponsored a series of highly successful negotiations to develop common guidelines for testing chemicals in its member countries.[162] These efforts led not only to uniform test guidelines for particular toxicological endpoints, such as carcinogenicity, but also to agreements about quality standards to be maintained in laboratory testing of chemicals (good laboratory practice). The OECD guidelines laid a foundation for mutual acceptance of test data and are likely to reduce the demand for costly duplicative testing.

Though a number of international agencies, including OECD, are interested in influencing national policies, the success of their harmonization efforts depends on striking a judicious balance between scientific and political decision-making. As long as they do not threaten the policy priorities of member states, international agencies can play a useful role in risk management, especially as a voice of reason in contentious areas of policy development. One organization that has successfully guarded itself against charges of intruding too deeply into policy is the International Agency for Research on Cancer (IARC). Its strategy has been to avoid making definitive statements in areas of real scientific uncertainty, recognizing that such statements inevitably lead to political controversy. In evaluating formaldehyde, for example, IARC took no definite position about the mouse cancer data, but concluded only that formaldehyde gas is carcinogenic to rats. IARC's cautious approach to evaluating carcinogens is also reflected in the agency's exclusive reliance on data already in the public domain, specifically, published articles in recognized journals.

A similar conservatism has marked IARC's approach to the issue of risk assessment.[163] Conscious of the need to improve the principles of carcinogenic risk assessment, IARC undertook in the early 1980s to review existing methodologies for quantitative analyses of epidemiological data. The agency has not endorsed any particular methodological approach, but is conducting a continuous review and updating of these methodologies to verify how far they can help in producing scientifically acceptable estimates of risk. The success of these strategies is evident in the respect that national regulatory authorities accord to IARC's determinations of carcinogenicity. The U.S. response to IARC has been especially noteworthy. Most U.S. agencies have now adopted the "weight of the evidence" approach recommended by IARC in evaluating carcinogenic hazards. Yet the international controversy over formaldehyde is just one example that indicates limits on IARC's power to defuse regulatory conflicts over chemicals of serious public concern.

When international organizations are openly perceived as making policy the result is not always successful, as in the case of OECD's efforts to secure agreement on a minimum premarket data (MPD) set in testing industrial chemicals.[164] Other institutions, notably some United Nations expert groups, have come much closer to harmonizing risk management policies for specific toxic substances, for example, by setting acceptable daily intakes (ADIs) for pesticides and food additives. But even these standards are viewed by many national governments as mere guidelines to be considered, but not necessarily adopted, in developing their own independent control strategies.[165]

Some experienced international administrators would like to see supranational organizations play a more active role in the policy aspects of risk management. Their argument is that beyond improving the efficiency of information exchange, the focus of most current harmonization activities, international organizations should also take up the challenge of systematizing decision-making procedures and promoting greater openness and responsibility in the deliberations of national expert groups. These suggestions are based on the view that international organizations are best placed to implement the shared goals and aspirations of technologically advanced societies. But in political terms these are distant visions. Few powerful national governments are ready to conform their regulatory processes and priorities to the demands of supranational agencies. Limiting such bodies to technical support functions seems more consistent with the desire of national agencies for maintaining maximum flexibility with respect to the assessment and management of risk.

The efforts of modern governments to regulate chemical carcinogens reveal deep-seated differences in national attitudes about the characterization and control of risk. The universality of science and its crucial role in risk regulation are recognized in all Western societies. Yet an examination of existing political and administrative frameworks indicates why science fails to exert a greater harmonizing influence on risk management. In dealing with uncertainty and expert conflicts, national regulatory systems take into account a host of interests besides the scientific community's views about risk. Cultural factors influence goals and priorities in risk management, as is evident from the varying emphasis on carcinogens in the regulatory systems of several European countries, Canada, and the United States. Different societies also respond differently to questions of political process and institutional design: Who should participate, how much should they know, how should disputes be resolved, and by what ultimate authority? The answers to these questions shape the assessment of uncertainty, overshadowing science and leading in the end to widely divergent policies for managing the same technological hazards.

Though there are many differences of detail among national programs for controlling carcinogens, the cases discussed in this monograph suggest that strategies for dealing with scientific uncertainty fall into three basic patterns. These are most clearly illustrated by varying national approaches to identifying carcinogens. The first approach, favored in West Germany (and, at the international level, by IARC), is to delegate the resolution of all scientific issues, including those marked by uncertainty, to technical experts. The responsible expert group then applies its own criteria to the interpretation of the evidence and explains its determinations with reference to these criteria. A second approach, best exemplified in British and Canadian decision-making, is to let determinations about carcinogenic risk emerge from a mixed scientific and administrative process, in which uncertainty is not always publicly analyzed. Carcinogens are targeted for action in Britain and Canada when a combination of scientific evidence and political pressure necessitates such action, but the government does not feel compelled to explain its analysis of the scientific and policy issues in explicit detail. Still a third approach, followed only in the United States, acknowledges that both scientific and political judgment are required in identifying carcinogens, but requires the political decision-maker to resolve conflicts caused by scientific uncertainty, generally in accordance with explicit agency guidelines.

The formaldehyde case study lends empirical support to the view that the third approach is least likely to produce closure in controversies about technological risk. Both IARC and Germany's DFG commission classified formaldehyde as a carcinogen without generating much controversy about the scientific validity of their classification criteria. Canadian authorities banned urea-formaldehyde foam insulation as a threat to public health, but did not become embroiled in scientific debate about the product's carcinogenicity. In Britain, a control limit was adopted for formaldehyde without significant elaboration of the scientific basis for this action. This outcome seems all the more remarkable since, by established British standards, the evidence of a human health risk from formaldehyde was weaker than is generally required to justify the adoption of a control limit. In the United States, by contrast, the carcinogenicity of formaldehyde was discussed in a wide variety of administrative and scientific forums. As a result, the scientific issues were probably more carefully analyzed in public in the United States than in any other country. But intellectual rigor was purchased at the price of political stalemate, and extensive discussion failed to produce the scientific or political consensus needed for decisive regulatory action.

Such protracted and inconclusive controversies lead one to question whether the U.S. preference for debating the scientific basis for risk management decisions in a public and adversarial setting is well advised. Certainly, the experience of other countries suggests that such conflicts can be avoided if both scientific and science policy issues are delegated to expert groups without any attempt to differentiate between them. Deciding uncertain scientific issues confidentially, without reference to principled policy guidelines, reduces technical controversy and leads to quicker government action. However, the cost of risk management by technical experts is that the public relinquishes control over important political and value choices. And decision-making without a requirement of public explanation not only invites the capture of governmental agencies by business interests, but encourages a relatively uncritical acceptance of science by lay participants in the risk management process. Thus, the alternatives to the U.S. approach do not fully resolve the problem of preserving democratic values in areas of mixed scientific and political decision-making.

Cross-national analysis of cancer policies helps illuminate some of the compromises that inevitably must be made in risk management. In particular, it appears that the goals of administrative efficiency and scientific credibility are incompatible with those of analytical rigor and informed public participation. However, understanding these trade-offs does not necessarily bring policy-makers closer to finding optimal "solutions" to problems of risk management. Variations in the cancer policies of several Western countries emphasize the extent to which decisions about risk are constrained by politics. In particular, the choice of institutions and procedures in each country is rooted in its individual political culture and cannot readily be modified, even if the costs are substantial. The indecisiveness of the U.S. approach, for example, may be bearable to many because what matters most in risk management is the process, not the outcome. Especially for nonindustrial interests in the United States, the opportunity to participate in varied forums and with full access to information may compensate for a decision-making process that often appears wavering and ineffectual.

The contrasting national approaches to risk management, and the absence of any "ideal" model for dispute resolution, open up several promising areas for comparative research. For policy analysts, the primary challenge is to evaluate the effectiveness of alternative institutional and procedural mechanisms for assessing and controlling risk. The contrasts between the United States and other countries suggest some obvious questions for future research. What is the impact of adversarial procedures on the production of relevant scientific information and on the clarity or rationality of administrative decision-making? Does extensive judicial review produce "better" decisions about risk? How do we know? Detailed comparative case studies offer one avenue for testing alternative hypotheses about these issues. But comparative policy analysis should also concern itself with studying the aggregate impact of risk management decisions, both qualitatively and quantitatively. How well do alternative policy structures achieve the fundamental goal of public protection and, equally important, at what cost? Most cross-national studies of regulation have focused on the initial formulation of policy, particularly the process of enacting legislation or setting regulatory standards. To assess the impact of policy, cross-national research should now devote much greater attention to patterns of enforcement and compliance and to feedback mechanisms that enable agencies to learn from their own mistakes. Areas of nongovernmental activity, such as voluntary standard-setting by hazardous industries, are also worth further study, since they form an important part of any country's package of mechanisms for reducing risk. Finally, more research is needed on the administrative and social costs of alternative regulatory approaches, particularly in the United States where rule-making often seems needlessly cumbersome and protracted.

Disparities in the assessment of risk by national and international expert bodies provide fruitful opportunities for advances in the sociology of knowledge. Specific cases, such as the history of the "cancer policy" or of formaldehyde regulation, create a basis for studying how social factors affect the interpretation of uncertainty and the certification of new scientific facts or theories. This monograph suggests that the processes by which scientific paradigms are produced and adopted in the policy context differ from comparable processes in traditional disciplinary settings. The creation and diffusion of knowledge in policy-relevant science thus merit study in their own right. Cultural factors bearing on the perception and analysis of risk can also be effectively studied in a cross-national context and may provide an interesting backdrop for research focusing more narrowly on the social construction of particular scientific claims.

Perhaps the richest area for further study, however, is the relationship between the politics of risk management and broader political processes in democratic societies. Comparative studies of risk regulation show the citizen in varying interactions with governmental, scientific, and corporate elites. Analyzing these patterns of involvement helps to elucidate concepts such as "participation" or "deference" that are central to our understanding of democratic political cultures. The processes devised by governments in Europe and North America to secure public input into risk management decisions suggest that the role of participation can be either too broadly or too narrowly conceived. The danger in the former case is governmental paralysis under overly insistent political demand; in the latter case, the threat is rather to the individual citizen's sense of competence in the increasingly significant sphere of technical decision-making. Striking the right balance between the uncomfortable polarities of public paralysis and private anomie is a pressing challenge for modern governments. Comparative studies of risk regulation may alert decision-makers to problems and possibilities that would not be disclosed through more ethnocentric approaches to policy analysis.

Notes

[1] Robert K. Merton, *The Sociology of Science* (Chicago: University of Chicago Press, 1973).

[2] Thomas S. Kuhn, *The Structure of Scientific Revolutions,* 2nd ed. (Chicago: University of Chicago Press, 1970).

[3] Mary Douglas, "Environments at Risk," in Jack Dowie and Paul Lefrere, eds., *Risk and Chance* (Milton Keynes, UK: Open University Press, 1980); *Purity and Danger* (London: Routledge & Kegan Paul, 1966); Mary Douglas and Aaron Wildavsky, *Risk and Culture* (Berkeley: University of California Press, 1982).

[4] Baruch Fischhoff, Sarah Lichtenstein, Paul Slovic, S. Derby, and R. Keeney, *Acceptable Risk* (New York: Cambridge University Press, 1981). See also J. P. Moatti, E. Stemmelen, and F. Fagnani, "Risk Perception, Social Conflicts and Acceptability of Technologies (An Overview of French Studies)," paper presented at the annual meeting of the Society for Risk Analysis, Knoxville, TN, September-October 1984.

[5] See, for example, Dorothy Nelkin, ed., *Controversy,* 2nd ed. (Beverly Hills, CA: Sage, 1984).

[6] Lennart J. Lundqvist, *The Hare and the Tortoise: Clean Air Policies in the United States and Sweden* (Ann Arbor: University of Michigan Press, 1980).

[7] Dorothy Nelkin and Michael Pollak, *The Atom Besieged* (Cambridge, MA: MIT Press, 1981).

[8] Steven Kelman, *Regulating America, Regulating Sweden: A Comparative Study of Occupational Safety and Health Policy* (Cambridge, MA: MIT Press, 1981).

[9] Howard Kunreuther, Joanne Linnerooth, and Rhonda Starnes, eds., *Liquefied Energy Gases Facility Siting: International Comparisons* (Laxenburg, Austria: International Institute for Applied Systems Analysis, 1982).

[10] David Vogel, "Cooperative Regulation: Environmental Protection in Great Britain," *Public Interest,* no. 72 (1983):88–106.

[11] Joseph L. Badaracco, "A Study of Adversarial and Cooperative Relationships Between Business and Government in Four Countries," report prepared for the Office of Technology, Strategy and Evaluation, U.S. Department of Commerce, Washington, DC, 1981; *Loading the Dice* (Cambridge, MA: Harvard Business School Press, 1985).

[12] Brendan Gillespie, Dave Eva, and Ron Johnston, "Carcinogenic Risk Assessment in the United States and Great Britain: The Case of Aldrin/Dieldrin," *Social Studies of Science* 9 (1979):265–301.

[13] Frances B. McCrea and Gerald E. Markle, "The Estrogen Replacement Controversy in the USA and UK: Different Answers to the Same Question?" *Social Studies of Science* 14 (1984):1–26.

[14] Ronald Brickman, Sheila Jasanoff, and Thomas Ilgen, *Controlling Chemicals: The Politics of Regulation in Europe and the United States* (Ithaca, NY: Cornell University Press, 1985).

[15] Alvin Weinberg, "Science and Trans-Science," *Minerva* 10 (1972):209.

[16] David Dickson, *The New Politics of Science* (New York: Pantheon Books, 1984).

[17] See, for example, Gabriel A. Almond and Sidney Verba, eds., *The Civic Culture Revisited* (Boston: Little, Brown, 1980).

[18] Susan Sontag, *Illness as Metaphor* (New York: Vintage Books, 1979).

[19] Rudyard Kipling, "The Wish House."

[20] W. H. Auden, "Miss Gee. A Ballad," from *Another Time, Poems* (New York: Random House, 1940). Reprinted by permission of Random House. Copyright © W. H. Auden, 1940, 1968.

[21] Nathan J. Karch, "Explicit Criteria and Principles for Identifying Carcinogens: A Focus of Controversy at the Environmental Protection Agency," in National Academy of Sciences/National Research Council, *Decision Making in the Environmental Protection Agency,* vol. 2a (Washington, DC: National Academy Press, 1977), pp. 119–206; Thomas O. McGarity, "Substantive and Procedural Discretion in Administrative Resolution of Science Policy Questions: Regulating Carcinogens in EPA and OSHA," *Georgetown Law Review* 67 (1979):729–810; and Sheila Jasanoff, "Science and the Limits of Administrative Rule-Making: Lessons from the OSHA Cancer Policy," *Osgoode Hall Law Journal* 20 (1982):536–61.

[22] U.S. Department of Labor, Occupational Safety and Health Administration, "Identification, Classification and Regulation of Potential Occupational Carcinogens," *Federal Register* 45 (January 22, 1980):5001–296.

[23] See Jasanoff, "Science and the Limits of Administrative Rule-Making."

[24] 21 U.S. Code §348(c)(3)(A).

[25] See Brickman et al., *Controlling Chemicals,* chaps. 2–5.

[26] European Chemical Industry Ecology and Toxicology Centre, "A Contribution to the Strategy for the Identification and Control of Occupational Carcinogens," Monograph no. 2, Brussels, September 1980.

27 Brickman et al., *Controlling Chemicals,* chaps. 2 and 8. Further, Cyril D. Burgess, "The Control of Carcinogens at Work," paper presented at the Bellagio Conference, "Scientific Information and Public Decision-Making on Toxic Chemicals," Bellagio, Italy, August 15–19, 1983.

28 Association of Scientific, Technical and Managerial Staffs, "The Prevention of Occupational Cancer," ASTMS Health and Safety Policy Series, no. 3, London, February 1980.

29 Royal Society, *Risk Assessment* (London: Royal Society, 1983), p. 166.

30 Brickman et al., *Controlling Chemicals,* pp. 208–9.

31 Ronald Brickman, Sheila Jasanoff, and Thomas Ilgen, *Chemical Regulation and Cancer: A Cross-National Study of Policy and Politics,* Report to the National Science Foundation (Cornell University, Ithaca, NY, 1982), p. 423.

32 Sven Hernberg, "Registration of Carcinogenic Exposures in Finland," paper presented at the Bellagio Conference, Bellagio, Italy, August 15–19, 1983.

33 Brickman et al., *Controlling Chemicals,* p. 83.

34 Liora Salter, "Science and Peer Review: The Canadian Standard-Setting Experience," *Science, Technology and Human Values* (forthcoming).

35 International Agency for Research on Cancer, *IARC Monographs on the Evaluation of the Carcinogenic Risk of Chemicals to Humans,* supplement 2 (Lyon: IARC, 1979).

36 Deutsche Forschungsgemeinschaft (DFG) Commission for Investigation of Health Hazards of Chemical Compounds in the Work Area, "Maximum Concentrations at the Workplace and Biological Tolerance Values for Working Materials 1982," Report no. 19 (Weinheim: Verlag Chemie, 1982).

37 DFG commission, "Maximum Concentrations at the Workplace," p. 51.

38 The DFG commission is regarded in Germany as an independent scientific body, though its members include scientists from both the universities and private industry. For a more detailed discussion of the commission's composition and the general role and nature of European expert groups, see Brickman et al., *Controlling Chemicals,* chap. 7.

39 See Gillespie et al., "Carcinogenic Risk Assessment," and Brickman et al., *Controlling Chemicals,* chap. 8 (comparing the regulation of 2,4,5-T in Britain, Germany, and the United States).

40 This committee was formed during the Carter Administration to coordinate the chemical regulatory policies of five agencies: EPA, OSHA, CPSC, the Food and Drug Administration (FDA), and the Food Safety and Quality Service of the U.S. Department of Agriculture.

41 Office of Science and Technology Policy, "Chemical Carcinogens: A Review of the Science and Its Associated Principles," *Federal Register* 50 (March 14, 1985):10371–442.

42 See Jasanoff, "Science and the Limits of Administrative Rule-Making," pp. 549–53.

43 Interview with Charles Gordon, OSHA, Washington, DC, 5 December 1980.

44 Eliot Marshall, "Revisions in Cancer Policy," *Science* 220 (April 1, 1983):36–37; Michael Wines, "Scandals at EPA May Have Done in Reagan's Move to Ease Cancer Control," *National Journal* 15 (June 18, 1983):1264–69.

45 Marshall, "Revisions in Cancer Policy." See also House Committee on Energy and Commerce, Subcommittee on Commerce, Transportation and Tourism, *Control of Carcinogens in the Environment,* 98th Cong., 1st Sess. (1983).

[46] Jasanoff, "Science and the Limits of Administrative Rule-Making," pp. 552–53.

[47] Interagency Regulatory Liaison Group, "Scientific Bases for Identification of Potential Carcinogens and Estimation of Risk," *Federal Register* 44, (July 6, 1979):39872.

[48] U.S. Department of Labor, "Identification, Classification and Regulation of Potential Occupational Carcinogens," pp. 5200–1.

[49] *Industrial Union Department, AFL-CIO* v. *American Petroleum Institute*, 448 U.S. 607 (1980).

[50] National Academy of Sciences/National Research Council, *Risk Assessment in the Federal Government: Managing the Process* (Washington, DC: National Academy Press, 1983).

[51] William Ruckelshaus, "Science, Risk, and Public Policy," *Science* 221 (1983): 1027–28. More recently, Ruckelshaus has acknowledged that there is no sharp dividing line between risk assessment and risk management. See, for example, "Risk in a Free Society," *Vital Speeches of the Day* 50 (1984):354–58.

[52] A. G. Ulsamer, K. C. Gupta, M. S. Cohn, and P. W. Preuss, "Formaldehyde in Indoor Air Toxicity and Risk," in House Committee on Science and Technology, Subcommittee on Investigations and Oversight, *Formaldehyde: Review of Scientific Basis of EPA's Carcinogenic Risk Assessment*, 97th Cong., 2d Sess. (1982), pp. 391–408.

[53] Environmental Protection Agency, "Proposed Guidelines for Carcinogen Risk Assessment: Request for Comments," *Federal Register* 49 (November 23, 1984): 46294–301.

[54] For general discussions of these problems, see EPA's proposed risk assessment guidelines cited in *n.*53. Further, see Office of Science and Technology Policy, "Chemical Carcinogens: Notice of Review of the Science and Its Associated Principles," *Federal Register* 49 (May 22, 1984):21594–661. For a European industrial view of risk assessment, see European Chemical Industry Ecology and Toxicology Centre, "Risk Assessment of Occupational Carcinogens," Monograph no. 3, Brussels, January 1982.

[55] Cass Peterson, "How Much Risk Is Too Much?" *Washington Post,* 4 February 1985, p. 8.

[56] Brent Barker, "Cancer and the Problems of Risk Assessment," *EPRI* (Electric Power Research Institute) *Journal* (December 1984):26–34 (see remarks of Karim Ahmed, representing the Natural Resources Defense Council).

[57] *Gulf South Insulation* v. *Consumer Product Safety Commission*, 701 F.2d 1137 (5th Cir., 1983).

[58] Relevant judicial decisions in the United States include *Industrial Union Department, AFL-CIO* v. *American Petroleum Institute*, 448 U.S. 607 (1980); *Monsanto* v. *Kennedy*, 613 F.2d 947 (DC Cir., 1979); *Alabama Power Co.* v. *Costle*, 606 F.2d 1068 (DC Cir., 1979).

[59] National Academy of Sciences/National Research Council, *Safety of Dams: Flood and Earthquake Criteria* (Washington, DC: National Academy Press, 1985), pp. 93–94. See also David A. Kessler, "Food Safety: Revising the Statute," *Science* 223 (1984):1037; and Eliot Marshall, "EPA Regulators Take on the Delaney Clause," *Science* 224 (1984):851.

[60] See, for example, Steven Kelman, "Cost-Benefit Analysis: An Ethical Critique," *Regulation* 5 (1981):33–39.

[61] See, for example, Chris Whipple, "Application of the De Minimis Concept in Risk Management," paper presented to a Joint Session of the American Nuclear Society and Health Physics Society, New Orleans, 6 June 1984.

[62] Royal Society, *Risk Assessment*, p. 23.

[63] Royal Society, *Risk Assessment*, p. 179.

[64] The tradition of turning to blue-ribbon expert committees, such as Royal Commissions, for policy guidance is well-entrenched in Britain. Such committees frequently address controversial questions of science policy. A recent example is the Warnock Committee's work on reproductive technologies. See Department of Health and Social Security, *Report of the Committee of Inquiry into Human Fertilisation and Embryology* (London: HMSO, 1984).

[65] Brickman et al., *Controlling Chemicals*, p. 209.

[66] Bellagio Conference, Bellagio, Italy, August 15–19, 1983.

[67] See, for example, McCrea and Markle, "The Estrogen Replacement Controversy," p. 15 and n. 96.

[68] The widely used multistage model for assessing cancer risks, for example, was developed by two British scientists. See P. Armitage and R. Doll, "Stochastic Models for Carcinogenesis," in L. Lecam and J. Neyman, eds., *Proceedings of the Fourth Berkeley Symposium on Mathematical Statistics and Probability* (Berkeley: University of California Press, 1961), pp. 19–38.

[69] See particularly Brickman et al., *Controlling Chemicals*, chaps. 7 and 8.

[70] Michael S. Baram, "Cost-Benefit Analysis: An Inadequate Basis for Health, Safety, and Environmental Regulatory Decisionmaking," *Ecology Law Quarterly* 8 (1980):409–72. See also *American Textile Manufacturers Inst. v. Donovan*, 452 U.S. 490 (1980).

[71] Interview, American Petroleum Institute, Washington, DC, 1984.

[72] Brickman et al., *Controlling Chemicals*, chap. 5.

[73] *Bushell* v. *Secretary of State for the Environment*, 3 W.L.R. 22 (1980).

[74] See *n.*41.

[75] Office of Science and Technology Policy, "Chemical Carcinogens," p. 10371.

[76] Environmental Protection Agency, "Proposed Guidelines for Carcinogen Risk Assessment," p. 46298.

[77] Richard Doll and Richard Peto, "The Causes of Cancer: Quantitative Estimates of Avoidable Risks of Cancer in the United States Today," *Journal of the National Cancer Institute* 66 (1981):1193–308.

[78] CPSC rule banning Tris, *Federal Register* 42 (June 1, 1977):28060–64.

[79] Arlene Blum and Bruce Ames, "Flame-Retardant Additives as Possible Cancer Hazards," *Science* 195 (1977):17–23.

[80] See, for example, "ICI Toxicologists Sound Note of Caution on Ames Test," *European Chemical News,* 17 February 1978, p. 24; Bruce Ames and Kim Hooper, "Does Carcinogenic Potential Correlate with Mutagenic Potency in the Ames Assay?" *Nature* 274 (1978):19–20; and John Ashby and J. A. Styles, "Factors Influencing Mutagenic Potency *in vitro*," *Nature* 274 (1978):20–22.

[81] Bruce Ames, "Dietary Carcinogens and Anticarcinogens," *Science* 221 (1983):1249–64.

[82] Bruce Ames, "Peanut Butter, Parsley, Pepper, and Other Carcinogens," *Wall Street Journal,* 14 February 1984, p. 32.

83 Samuel S. Epstein, *The Politics of Cancer* (Garden City, NY: Anchor Books, 1979).

84 Epstein, *The Politics of Cancer,* p. 1261; see also Barker, "Cancer and the Problems of Risk Assessment."

85 *Science* 221 (September 23, 1983): cover.

86 Douglas, "Environments at Risk," p. 290.

87 Kuhn, *The Structure of Scientific Revolutions,* pp. 25–34.

88 Jasanoff, "Science and the Limits of Administrative Rule-Making," pp. 554–56.

89 For a claim that scientific uncertainty is socially constructed even outside the policy setting, see Trevor J. Pinch, "The Sun-Set: The Presentation of Uncertainty in Scientific Life," *Social Studies of Science* 11 (1981):131–58.

90 Frederica Perera and Catherine Petito, "Formaldehyde: A Question of Cancer Policy," *Science* 216 (1982):1285–91.

91 W. D. Kerns, K. L. Pavkov, D. J. Donofrio, E. J. Gralla, and J. A. Swenberg, "Carcinogenicity of Formaldehyde in Rats and Mice after Long-Term Inhalation Exposure," *Cancer Research* 43 (1983):4382–91.

92 International Agency for Research on Cancer, *IARC Monographs on the Evaluation of the Carcinogenic Risk of Chemicals to Humans,* vol. 29 (Lyon: IARC, 1982).

93 DFG commission, "Maximum Concentrations at the Workplace."

94 Interview, *Health and Safety Executive,* August 1984.

95 Personal communication from Cyril Burgess, Health and Safety Executive, 28 March 1985.

96 The British Health and Safety at Work Act imposes a general duty on employers "to ensure, so far as is reasonably practicable, the health, safety and welfare at work of all . . . employees."

97 For an account of these events, see David S. Cohen, "Public and Private Law Dimensions of the UFFI Problem," unpublished paper on file at Faculty of Law, University of British Columbia, 23 October 1982. An abbreviated version of this paper has been published in *Canadian Business Law Journal* 8 (1984):309–43, 410–48.

98 See Bureau of National Affairs, *International Environment Reporter,* Current Report, 14 January 1981, pp. 604–5, and 13 May 1981, pp. 845–46.

99 *Gulf South Insulation* v. *Consumer Product Safety Commission,* 701 F.2d 1137 (5th Cir., 1983).

100 Nicholas Ashford, C. William Ryan, and Charles Caldart, "A Hard Look at Federal Regulation of Formaldehyde: A Departure from Reasoned Decisionmaking," *Harvard Environmental Law Review* 7 (1983):297–370.

101 Environmental Protection Agency, "Formaldehyde: Determination of Significant Risk; Advance Notice of Proposed Rulemaking and Notice," *Federal Register* 49 (May 23, 1984):21870–97.

102 For a concise summation of these arguments, see statement of Richard Griesemer, *Formaldehyde Hearing,* 97th Cong., 2d Sess. (1982), pp. 57–66.

103 See, for example, statement of Norton Nelson, *Formaldehyde Hearing,* 97th Cong., 2d Sess. (1982), pp. 30–31.

104 Gibson, *Formaldehyde Hearing,* p. 213.

105 Environmental Protection Agency, "Formaldehyde," p. 21874.

[106] Bellagio Conference, Bellagio, Italy, August 15–19, 1983.

[107] Nicholas Ashford, C. William Ryan, and Charles Caldart, "Law and Science Policy in Federal Regulation of Formaldehyde," *Science* 222 (1983):895.

[108] There are, of course, numerous possible tests for deciding whether an issue is "scientific." McCray, for example, describes three distinct uses for the term "scientific." See Lawrence E. McCray, "An Anatomy of Risk Assessment: Scientific and Extra-Scientific Components in the Assessment of Scientific Data on Cancer Risks," in National Academy of Sciences/National Research Council, *Risk Assessment in the Federal Government: Managing the Process,* Working Papers (Washington, DC: National Academy Press, 1983), p. 94. For our purposes, however, the important point is that under *any* use of the term "scientific," disagreements may arise about whether a specific issue is scientific. The term's ambiguity merely opens the door to more numerous controversies.

[109] See Ashford, Ryan, and Caldart, "Law and Science Policy in Federal Regulation of Formaldehyde."

[110] Toxic Substances Control Act, 15 U.S. Code §2603(f) [or TSCA §4(f)].

[111] *Formaldehyde Hearing,* 97th Cong., 2d Sess. (1982), p. 23.

[112] Ashford, Ryan, and Caldart, "Law and Science Policy in Federal Regulation of Formaldehyde," pp. 896–97.

[113] Bureau of National Affairs, "Current Developments," in *Daily Labor Report,* 25 August 1982, pp. A-9–A-10.

[114] *International Union, United Auto Workers* v. *Donovan,* 590 F.Supp. 747 (D.C.D.C., 1984).

[115] *Natural Resources Defense Council* v. *Ruckelshaus,* no. 83-2039 (D.C.D.C., July 19, 1983).

[116] National Center for Toxicological Research, *Formaldehyde Consensus Report* (Washington, DC 1984).

[117] Formaldehyde Institute, "Comments on EPA's Formaldehyde ANPR," Appendix B, Docket no. OPTS 62033 (Washington, DC, 23 July 1984), pp. 20–25.

[118] *Federal Register* 49 (1984):12877.

[119] Occupational Safety and Health Administration, "Occupational Exposure to Formaldehyde," *Federal Register* 50 (December 10, 1985):50412–99.

[120] See David L. Bazelon, "Risk and Responsibility," *Science* 205 (1979):277–80.

[121] See Karch, "Explicit Criteria."

[122] See, for example, American Industrial Health Council, "AIHC Proposal for a Science Panel," mimeographed, March 1981; "Proposals for Improving the Science Base for Chronic Health-Hazard Decision-Making (Scarsdale, NY: AIHC, December 1981).

[123] See, for example, Organisation for Economic Cooperation and Development, *Technology on Trial* (Paris: OECD, 1979); and Stephen McCaffrey and Robert Lutz, eds., *Environmental Pollution and Individual Rights* (Deventer, The Netherlands: Kluwer, 1978).

[124] See, for example, *Greater Boston TV* v. *FCC,* 444 F.2d 841 (D.C. Cir., 1970); *International Harvester Co.* v. *Ruckelshaus,* 478 F.2d 615 (D.C. Cir., 1973); and *Ethyl Corp.* v. *EPA,* 541 F.2d 1, at 68–69 (D.C. Cir., 1976).

[125] For example, see Nicholas Ashford, "Advisory Committees in OSHA and EPA: Their Use in Regulatory Decisionmaking," *Science, Technology and Human Values* 9 (1984):72–82.

[126] Brian Wynne, *Rationality and Ritual* (Chalfont St. Giles, UK: British Society for the History of Science, 1982).

[127] One exception is the lively lobbying effort orchestrated by the Campaign on Freedom of Information in Britain in 1984. To date, however, the campaign has not met with success in Parliament.

[128] For a discussion of these legal doctrines in the context of public interest litigation, see Eckard Rehbinder, "Private Recourse for Environmental Harm—Federal Republic of Germany," in McCaffrey and Lutz, *Environmental Pollution and Individual Rights.*

[129] Brickman et al., *Controlling Chemicals,* chap. 2.

[130] Badaracco, "A Study of Adversarial and Cooperative Relationships."

[131] Sheila Jasanoff, "Negotiation or Cost-Benefit Analysis: A Middle Road for U.S. Policy?" *Environmental Forum* 2 (1983):37–43.

[132] David Vogel, *National Styles of Regulation* (Ithaca, NY: Cornell University Press, 1986).

[133] Brickman et al., *Controlling Chemicals,* pp. 162–66.

[134] Liora Salter, "Observations on the Politics of Assessment: The Captan Case," *Canadian Public Policy* 11 (1985):64–76.

[135] Interview with Sheila McKechnie, ASTMS, London, August 1984.

[136] This paragraph incorporates the conclusions of the working group that reported on the issue of consensus at the Bellagio Conference, Bellagio, Italy, August 15–19, 1983.

[137] Cohen, "Public and Private Law Dimensions," chap. 2, pp. 4–10.

[138] Cohen, "Public and Private Law Dimensions," p. 8.

[139] Health and Safety Executive, Guidance Note EH40, May 1980.

[140] Nicholas Ashford, "Advisory Committees in OSHA and EPA," p. 75.

[141] See, for example, *Industrial Union Department, AFL-CIO v. Hodgson,* 499 F.2d 467 (D.C. Cir., 1974); *Lead Industries Association Inc. v. EPA,* 647 F.2d 1130 (D.C. Cir., 1980). Also see David L. Bazelon, "Coping with Technology Through the Legal Process," *Cornell Law Review* 62 (1977):817–32.

[142] Philip Harter, "Negotiating Regulations: A Cure for the Malaise," *Environmental Impact Assessment Review* 3 (1982):75–92.

[143] The following account is based on interviews with one of the mediators (Philip Harter) and with representatives of the American Petroleum Institute and AFL-CIO, Washington, DC, September and December 1984.

[144] Occupational Safety and Health Administration, "Occupational Exposure to Benzene," *Federal Register* 50 (December 10, 1985):50512–86.

[145] A recent illustration of this phenomenon was the settlement agreement drawn up between several manufacturers of the herbicide Agent Orange and the class of Vietnam veterans claiming health injuries from wartime exposure to the substance. Scientific uncertainty was a major factor motivating the settlement. See *In Re "Agent Orange" Product Liability Litigation,* 597 F.Supp. 740 (E.D.N.Y., 1984).

[146] Interview with Peg Seminario, AFL-CIO, Washington, DC, 1984.

[147] Gabriel A. Almond and Sidney Verba, *The Civic Culture* (Princeton, NJ: Princeton University Press, 1963).

[148] Almond and Verba, p. 493.

[149] Almond and Verba, p. 484.

[150] Wynne notes that although environmentalists participated at the Windscale Inquiry, the general public "appeared either indifferent or disoriented." *Rationality and Ritual,* p. 169.

[151] In the U.S. context, for example, negotiation may be a more useful strategy for resolving disputes about legislative policy and administrative priorities rather than control standards for specific chemicals. Thus, a "successful" outcome was recently reported to negotiations between the chemical industry and a coalition of environmental, labor, and consumer groups on proposed changes in the law regulating pesticides. See Philip Shabecoff, "Industry and Environment Groups Reach Accord on Pesticides Curb," *New York Times,* 12 September 1985, p. A20.

[152] I am indebted to Brian Wynne for this observation.

[153] Personal communication from Julian Peto, 6 September 1983.

[154] For a more extensive discussion of this point, see Sheila Jasanoff, "Peer Review in the Regulatory Process," *Science, Technology and Human Values* 10 (1985):20–32. See also American Chemical Society and Conservation Foundation, "Guidelines for Peer Review of the Scientific Basis for Regulatory Decisions," unpublished paper (1985).

[155] See Sheila Jasanoff, "The Misrule of Law at OSHA," in Dorothy Nelkin, ed., *The Language of Risk* (Beverly Hills, CA: Sage, 1985), p. 160.

[156] Lawrence McCray, "An Anatomy of Risk Assessment," pp. 90–95.

[157] See Ashford, Ryan, and Caldart, "Law and Science Policy in Federal Regulation of Formaldehyde." See also McGarity, "Substantive and Procedural Discretion."

[158] See statement of John Todhunter, *Formaldehyde Hearing,* 97th Cong., 2d Sess. (1982), pp. 140–41.

[159] For example, EPA must consult with a committee of external scientific reviewers in the course of rulemaking under the Clean Air Act as well as under the Federal Insecticide, Fungicide, and Rodenticide Act.

[160] Jasanoff, "Peer Review in the Regulatory Process."

[161] Brickman et al., *Controlling Chemicals,* pp. 305–8.

[162] Joanne K. Nichols and Peter J. Crawford, *Managing Chemicals in the 1980s* (Paris: Organisation for Economic Cooperation and Development, 1983).

[163] One exception to this approach was IARC's brief foray into quantitative risk assessment for workers exposed to benzene. The incident created an international controversy and IARC withdrew its preliminary quantitative estimate from the final monograph on benzene. See Marjorie Sun, "Risk Estimate Vanishes from Benzene Report," *Science* 217 (1982):914–15.

[164] See Brickman et al., *Controlling Chemicals,* chap. 11.

[165] Brickman et al., *Controlling Chemicals,* chap. 11.